THRIVING
YOUTH MINISTRY
IN SMALLER CHURCHES

secrets for cultivating a dynamic youth ministry

BY
RICK CHROMEY
+ STEPHANIE CARO

Thriving Youth Ministry in Smaller Churches
Secrets for Cultivating a Dynamic Youth Ministry

Credits
Authors: Rick Chromey & Stephanie Caro
Executive Developer: Nadim Najm
Chief Creative Officer: Joani Schultz
Assistant Editor: Rob Cunningham
Cover Art Director: Jeff Storm
Designer: Veronica Lucas
Production Manager: DeAnne Lear

Unless otherwise indicated, all Scripture quotations are taken from the Holy Bible,
New Living Translation, copyright © 1996, 2004, 2007. Used by permission of
Tyndale House Publishers, Inc., Carol Stream, Illinois 60188. All rights reserved.

Library of Congress Cataloging-in-Publication Data
Chromey, Rick.
   Thriving youth ministry in smaller churches : secrets for cultivating
a dynamic youth ministry / [authors, Rick Chromey and Stephanie Caro].
      p. cm.
   ISBN 978-0-7644-4051-9 (pbk. : alk. paper)
   1. Church group work with youth--United States. 2. Small
churches--United States. I. Caro, Stephanie. II. Title.
   BV4447.C484 2009
   259'.230973--dc22   2009043292

10 9 8 7 6   17 16 15 14 13
Printed in the United States of America.

TABLE OF CONTENTS

DEDICATION 1

ACKNOWLEDGEMENTS 3

INTRODUCTION 5

CHAPTER ONE: SMALL IS TALL! 11

CHAPTER TWO: WAKE UP AND SMELL THE CHANGE 25

CHAPTER THREE: GROWING TALL WHILE STAYING SMALL . . . 45

CHAPTER FOUR: SCRATCH YOUR NICHE 65

CHAPTER FIVE: DING! YOU'RE NOW FREE
TO MOVE ABOUT THE KINGDOM 85

CHAPTER SIX: FISH STICKS! 111

CHAPTER SEVEN: FIRE STARTERS! 137

CHAPTER EIGHT: FACEBOOK ROCKS! 153

CHAPTER NINE: CHA CHA SUNDAY SCHOOL 175

CHAPTER TEN: WISH UPON A STARFISH 201

CHAPTER ELEVEN: DYNO-MITES! 229

POSTSCRIPT 249

DEDICATION

To all the smaller churches that never get a dedication page in a book. This one's for *you*.

—*Rick Chromey*

I would like to dedicate this book to my dad, in memory of 40+ years of faithful ministry to smaller churches, and in honor of the youth at St. James UMC in St. Pete, FL.

—*Stephanie Caro*

ACKNOWLEDGMENTS

This is that special space to thank everyone who made me who I am and essentially created this work. To be honest, that list would be long and laborious (and I would no doubt leave someone out). So I'll just keep it short and sweet.

First of all, I am deeply grateful to God for not giving up on me. Without Jesus, my life would be empty and vain. I'm also thankful for my home church (First Christian Church) in Lewistown, Montana, especially to my youth leaders and pastors who saw something in me that I did not. I'm equally deeply indebted to those who have recently shaped my life and stretched my world, particularly my friend Dr. Leonard Sweet. Len, you have ruined me for life. I love you.

I'd also like to thank all my students over the past 15 years from Boise Bible College, Saint Louis Christian College, and Kentucky Christian University. You made me a better professor and person. I pray you remember me for the good, forgive my bad, and always serve the king and the kingdom.

A special word of gratitude to all my friends and family at Group Publishing for making this book a reality, especially Nadim Najm and my editor Rob Cunningham. I have been marked by R.E.A.L. learning philosophy, and I'm proud to be part of the Group family and have friends like Thom and Joani Schultz, Rick Lawrence, and Chris Yount-Jones (to name a few). I am also indebted to Stephanie Caro, who agreed to walk beside me in this journey and offer additional insights and ideas. While I'm glad she agreed with most of my material, I'm also thankful for her disagreements and expansions of thought. This book isn't about me but about you. Stephanie brings you into the trenches of smaller church youth ministry. She's been my hands and feet.

Finally, I must confess a deep, undying gratitude to my own family. To my wife, Patti, I want to thank you for being a writer's widow. It's not a glamorous life, and I am forever grateful for allowing me to travel, speak, and bleed on paper. You have sacrificed much for my dreams and now I hope to do the same for you. Dinner dishes are on me. To my children, Rebecca and Ryan, I have similar sentiments. I am so fortunate to have kids like you who love Jesus and his church. Rebecca, I pray all your composing dreams also come true, and Ryan, keep rocking for The Rock. You are my inspiration.

To everyone else…*thanks.*

INTRODUCTION

Everywhere you look the American church is in trouble. Just listen to a few of these clarion calls of alarm:

"...the church in America is not booming. It is in crisis. On any given Sunday, the vast majority of Americans are absent from church. Even more troublesome, as the American population continues to grow, the church falls further and further behind." (David T. Olson, *The American Church in Crisis.*)

"A growing number of people are leaving the institutional church for a new reason. They are not leaving because they have lost faith. They are leaving the church to preserve their faith." (Reggie McNeal, *The Present Future.*)

"Americans today are more devoted to seeking spiritual enlightenment than at any previous time during the twentieth century. Yet, at this moment of optimum opportunity, Christianity is having less impact on people's perspectives and behaviors than ever. Why is that? Because a growing majority of people have dismissed the Christian faith as weak, outdated, and irrelevant." (George Barna, *The Second Coming of the Church.*)

Ouch. Talk about taking one on the church chin. Weak. Outdated. Irrelevant. And yet, the statistics don't betray those attitudes. All you have to do is review the headlines:

Most religious groups in USA have lost ground, survey finds[1]

Poll: Catholics waver on faith, but like the pope[2]

Americans freely change or drop, their religion[3]

Half of all Baptist churches could be gone by 2030[4]

[1] usatoday.com/news/religion/2009-03-09-american-religion-ARIS_N.htm?csp=DailyBriefing
[2] usatoday.com/news/religion/2008-04-13-catholic-poll_N.htm
[3] religions.pewforum.org/?loc=interstitialskip
[4] faithinfocus.wordpress.com/2009/06/25/understanding-the-southern-baptist-convention/

More than 50,000 women have left the church annually in the past two decades.[5]

The end of Christian America (Newsweek cover)[6]

All these statistics and studies reveal a few insightful truths. **First, the world has changed but the church is stuck.** Christianity—those who follow Christ—continues to grow but "churchianity" is clearly on the decline. The church culture is out of step with wider society and our message no longer resonates. For some this might be a badge of honor (*"Good! We're supposed to be counter-cultural and not-of-this-world"*) but I believe this is reckless and questionable biblical application. We can't on one hand "separate" from the world and on the other hand fulfill the Great "Go-Mission" to "enter into the world" and make disciples (Matthew 28:18-20). Jesus didn't. Peter and Paul didn't. Countless saints throughout history didn't. Relevance isn't always evil, but obsolescence is always deadly.

Second, the future church will thrive in being small. The mainline, middle, and mainstream are dying and splintering into countless fragments. Micro is the new mega. Small is big. Scripture clearly roots for the underdog. David against Goliath. A boy with fish and bread. Mustard seeds. As you'll discover in the coming chapters, being smaller is a huge advantage. We'll just have to think differently about what that looks like—much differently.

Finally, it's time to recapture the heart of a generation. In 25 years of powerful youth ministry resources, programming, teen curricula, edgy conferences, and national conventions, the product we've produced is frightening. As Christian Smith documented in his exhaustive study of teenagers, most have swallowed "moralistic therapeutic deism" as their theology. *Be good and you'll make it to heaven. God is like a genie if you're in need, but he's not all that interested in our pitiful, petty lives.* It's hardly the God revealed within Scripture, and that's why you are so important. Youth ministry is the last chance a church gets to save, salve, and serve.

[5]foxnews.com/story/0,2933,410581,00.html
[6]newsweek.com/id/192583?GT1=43002

As youth leaders we have a great responsibility, for if we fail, the church of tomorrow is weaker for it.

When I wrote this book back in 1990 for Group, we called it *Youth Ministry in Small Churches*. It was a good title and a successful book for nearly two decades. But times have changed and so have I. That's why this book is completely new. It's some of my freshest thoughts—which in another 20 years might be frightening! I'll be honest, finding a title for this work wasn't easy. We debated it widely. I asked my Facebook friends for suggestions. Even after the book was nearly finished we were still hashing out how to boil it down to one concise, engaging, and attractive statement. We finally landed on *Thriving Youth Ministry in Smaller Churches: Secrets for Cultivating a Dynamic Youth Ministry*.

I think it says it all.

In the digital world of the 21st century—or 21C, as you'll see throughout this book—we can create a thriving youth ministry. It's only "secret" because to get there you'll have to check a lot of your youth ministry luggage at the door. Business as usual won't cut it. Copycat programs and cheap imitations won't get it done. The smaller church is the perfect place to develop disciples, deepen learning, create change, and unleash leaders. You see, I'm a product of a small church in central Montana. When I was growing up we didn't have a youth minister. Rather our church made ministers of every youth. I debuted my artistic talent on stage around age 8, doing a pastel chalk drawing of heaven while the pastor preached. I led corporate worship as a middle schooler, lip-synching my way through the songs due to a changing voice. I preached my first sermon at 13. It's no wonder I gravitated toward pastoral ministries and church leadership.

I'll be honest. I think we've lost a lot in attempts to entertain teenagers into the kingdom. Last night at our youth group I watched adults insanely work to keep students engaged, behaving, and having fun. We played a game where teenagers wrote compliments on the backs of friends. Several wrote on my back statements like: "U R Cool." "Baldy." "Funny." Or "good teacher." My favorite was from a hyper teenager named Isaac who simply wrote: "I love you."

I'll confess that most of the comments were lame, and I'll even admit today's generation doesn't know how to compliment (all they see in the media and personally experience is criticism, complaint, and condemnation). I get it. But when a goofy kid tells you he "loves" me, it fires my jets.

You see, a lot of people think I'm too old for youth ministry. I've pursued a few jobs in larger congregations and quickly learned I wasn't "hip" enough. Obviously, I don't wear Aéropostale, listen to Taylor Swift, or watch all the TV shows teenagers love, but that's OK. It's only another reason why I love the smaller church. It even has a place for us "old salty dog" types. When I think back on my favorite youth leaders they were all over 35 and in various states of physical decline (balding, fat, gray, wrinkled). One couple smoked like a furnace. Of course we all knew it and they told us to stay away from tobacco, but I found their authenticity attractive. If God could love a leathery, smelly chain-smoker then I had a shot, too. And so do you.

I hope you'll read this book this way.

Loopy.

You heard me, right. *Loopy.* Each chapter is unique and stands on its own, so don't be afraid to start in the middle or at the end. Read a chapter a dozen times or three times or once. But read it slow. Let the ideas and insights marinate. Get out a pen and write yourself notes. Highlight favorite statements. And don't be afraid to argue with me. Go ahead and write your disagreements, agitations, or confusion in the margins. Make this book come alive. When you're finished with a chapter find someone with whom you can "talk it out." Conversation is key to change. When we read a book in isolation we lose.

I've asked Stephanie Caro, a small church youth worker, to join me in this journey. You'll love Stephanie! She's been around the block a few times in youth ministry. Between the two of us we have over 50 years logged in youth work. We hope that earns us a little respect, but if not, we can take it. Stephanie has done a masterful job in adding ideas and insights, implications and applications. She'll take my thoughts and give them wings.

You'd do well to listen to her, and I certainly encourage joining her online discussions on small church youth ministry.

Let me break this book down into four simple statements. It's about giving you the GOLD. Youth ministry in a 21C culture is different, and those who lead teenagers will need to adopt and adapt a GOLDen lens.

Grace
Organism
Loopy
Decentralized

In a nutshell, a thriving youth ministry will be immersed in grace (unconditional love and acceptance, surprise, and delight). It will be a fluid and flexible organism that changes year-to-year, month-to-month, and even Sunday-to-Sunday. It will also be loopy in its feedback, leaning upon multiple evaluation tools. And finally, the power will flow from the edges to the middle rather than vice versa. If that sounds like a smaller church in context, you're right. The smaller congregation is perfectly sized for fluidity, feedback, and freedom.

If you think about it, traditional youth ministry in most churches today is exactly the opposite. It's about conforming to rules and using incentives (prizes, food, and even money) to get students to do what they wouldn't normally do. Youth programs are highly mechanized and formulaic, led by a few solitary adults and tied to strict schedules and discipleship curriculum. Students rarely lead, except perhaps to play in the band or do a pet service project. Little to no evaluation happens to confirm effectiveness. In the majority of youth ministries today, the power flows from a single person, adult team, or office.

It's no wonder the church is losing attraction value—but it doesn't have to. The future of the church need not be bleak or weak, full of fear or frustration. With God all things are possible. With God the dead can rise. With God the storms can still. With God the blind can see.

That's what we need to thrive. Life. Purpose. Vision.
My hope is this book is the catalyst for change.
My desire is a teenager will lead the church.

My dream is that smaller congregations will grow great in influence. My vision is for a mustard seed revolution.

In some ways this is a dangerous book. You may feel the bite or cut or scrape of a well-placed point. Just go with the sting. No pain, no gain, right? And if the title doesn't suit you, that's fine, too. Make up your own. Change the chapter titles to suit our own imagination. This book is ultimately about you, your church, and your students.

So let's go.

And I'll see you on the other side.

CHAPTER ONE ◎ SMALL IS TALL!

> *"You don't have enough faith," Jesus told them. "I tell you the truth, if you had faith even as small as a mustard seed, you could say to this mountain, 'Move from here to there,' and it would move. Nothing would be impossible"*
> *(Matthew 17:20 NLT).*
>
> *"We can do no great things, only small things with great love."*
> *(Mother Teresa)*

Sometimes the best ideas pop up in the strangest of places—like Los Angeles rush hour traffic. As a city dweller, I'm no stranger to slowdowns, but it was during a particularly sticky car creep in Los Angeles that a rich insight dented my imagination.

Maybe it was because everywhere I looked there were vehicles moving at the speed of slug. Luxury cars. Big-rig trucks. Sports cars. Delivery vans. Pickups. SUVs. Nobody was going anywhere fast, and most drivers seemed oblivious to the general lack of movement. People were fiddling with their radios, checking their makeup, gulping down a sandwich—and I saw more than one driver actually reading a book. We were all trapped like fly-papered gnats to this asphalt molasses, inching along like a sea of taillights glowing red against the Southern California horizon.

And then it happened: A motorcyclist whizzed by my window, scooted between the cars ahead, and quickly disappeared. Then another passed to my right, and another, and yet another. We were stuck, but these two-wheelers sailed by unscathed and undeterred with the slowdown. Yes, it was risky to steer and cruise between the cars, but I watched in amazement as they effortlessly left me sucking on diesel fumes and watching my gas tank drain.

That's when it hit me: *"Small is tall."* When traffic stalls or stops, the smaller you are, the greater advantage you possess. You can change lanes faster and more frequently. You can weave and work your way forward better. I'd rather be driving a Toyota than a tractor trailer in a traffic jam. And when traffic breaks loose and speeds forward, the smaller vehicles clearly win the rat race, leaving the large trucks to grind their gears.

Small is tall in an ever-changing, rapid, fluid culture, too.

The smaller you are, the more possibility you possess to navigate the jams that define contexts and the changes that impact our current culture.

A CULTURAL SHIFTING

I love taking trips with teenagers. When I wrote this chapter I was headed back to Boise from a youth leadership conference I hadn't attended in years. The week was soaked in metaphor and story about how to "Move," using Moses and the Hebrew slaves as a storyboard. Worship was experiential and celebratory, featuring streamers, balloons, hand-washing, and hugs. Students rushed the stage whenever the band played. Visual media told the stories of the Exodus in clever formats while speakers incorporated teen humor, culture, and social situations to make their points. Each day concluded with a "move" moment where teenagers expressed commitments verbally and relationally.

I was surprised how much this conference had changed.

Do you remember 1985? I do.

The Reagan revolution was in full swing, and the millennial generation was in operation birth mode. A generational shift was in the air.

"Prepare to feel obsolete. It's the first step to moving ahead."

—Elizabeth Weil, youth culture writer (Quoted by Leonard Sweet in *Carpe Mañana)*

"Baby On Board" signs on minivans announced a new attitude. On television, *The Cosby Show* and *Family Ties* struck a nerve. In 1985, Coca-Cola changed its formula to "new" Coke and quickly discovered "classic" was a better sell. Meanwhile a strange new computer was making noise—the Apple Macintosh, introduced a year earlier. It was the opening of the personal computing window.

Something was also happening in the church. A boomer generation tired of sowing its wild oats with '70s permissiveness pursued a spiritual awakening that spawned a New Age movement and "megachurch" emergence in places like Willow Creek and Saddleback. The boomer generation that returned to church brought a desire for fresh worship (praise songs vs. hymns), relevant preaching topics, and quality youth and children's ministries.

What few realized was something even deeper was also happening. It wasn't just a normal generational shifting but a cataclysmic cultural earthquake. Everything was about to change, and technology was the epicenter, particularly emerging "mega-techs" like the cellular phone and the Internet.

The mid-'80s technology was still primitive by today's standards. Televisions and phones were tethered to cable and cord. Personal music was a cassette in a Sony Walkman. Popular video games included Galaga or Pac-Man (though an upstart named Nintendo was catching on). The digital revolution remained a future, unseen reality. Few people a quarter century ago could imagine downloads, file sharing, web surfing, texting, IMing, MP3s, JPEGs, GPS, DVR, or e-mail. Who could imagine a cell phone "computer" that could record an event and instantly communicate it to the world?

Who could imagine playing a video game so realistic you could hurt yourself physically? Who could imagine watching movies in your car or live television at 30,000 feet?

Who could imagine that wireless and web technology could alter and rearrange cultural dialects? Television helped ignite the tech revolution in the 1960s. By 1985, technology had effectively moved our culture from a Gutenberg word-based world into a multi-visual experience where story, metaphor, and parable became "eye-deas." In 1981, music television (MTV) was born but it would take Michael Jackson's *Thriller* video to change the genre into story. The World Wide Web found its cultural traction in 1994 when Netscape opened the portal for average Joes and Janes to "surf the Web." The cell phone was a novelty item for the rich and famous, but it eventually found a tipping point with the masses. In fact, the year 2000 marked a socio-techno shifting as the whole world went "flat" (according to columnist and author Thomas Friedman). I would further add that the world has gone F-A-T. Fluid. Accessible. Temporary.

In less than a decade, our world evolved from a modern mechanical machine to a postmodern hyper-relational body. Suddenly one size didn't fit all. Everything was different. You could *feel* it.

David is a typical teenager. Sit with him at lunch and his cell phone buzzes text alerts as he chats about the latest YouTube video or iTunes song he downloaded. David's world is highly personalized. He lives by his iPod's playlist, creating music for every mood, situation, or occasion. David's world is a mouse click away. He buys, learns, connects, researches, maps, and shares secrets online.

In his free time he creates digital videos, plays online games, and searches for new friends on Facebook. In David's world everything is fluid. Everything connects, converses, and communes.

David's world is also amazingly accessible. It's 24/7/365. His cell phone and web connection create instant communication. When Michael Jackson died, David didn't hear the news from NBC or CNN but from his Facebook phone feed. He routinely texts his friends during church with encouraging thoughts, insights, and applications he's learning from the sermon. David finds his answers on life by searching Google or by texting "ChaCha" for the answer. David never gets lost when driving, thanks to a GPS gift from his folks. He never misses a television show. If he forgets to DVR, he just heads to Hulu to catch the episode. Finally, this new world has made everyone a publisher, including David, who blogs on his favorite blues artists and posts his own ideas on the Bible at various online discussion boards.

Of course, all this change has its edge and consequence. For David, it's created a temporary and disposable culture. He'll pay $3 to drink water from plastic but knows that bottle will take eternity to decompose. He's lost more than one paper for failure to "save," and one time his failure to back up a hard drive cost him thousands of precious photographs and videos. For David, his greatest fear was a fatal error message until he discovered online storage "in a cloud" at Carbonite. David changes e-mail addresses and passwords routinely.

David lives in a completely different world than most adults over 35 experienced as teenagers. He loves Jesus but finds church boring compared to his life.

"If the prospect of this flattening—and all of the pressures, dislocations, and opportunities accompanying it—causes you unease about the future, you are not alone nor wrong. Whenever civilization has gone through one of these disruptive, dislocating technological revolutions—like Gutenberg's introduction of the printing press— the whole world has changed in profound ways. But there is something about the flattening of the world that is going to be qualitatively different from other such profound changes: the speed and breadth with which it is taking hold."

—Thomas L. Friedman, journalist and author *The World is Flat: A Brief History of the Twenty-First Century*

It's hard to sit still for an hour listening to others sing, talk, and serve. His smaller church of 125 tries to be relevant with PowerPoint sermons and praise songs, but he still feels disconnected. He senses God's presence the most when he's serving soup for the homeless or riding his bike or playing his guitar (all of which he does on his own outside of his church).

David hungers to know God and to have a relationship with Jesus. He just doesn't see why he has to go to church to have that connection. After all, in his wireless world he has instant access and immediate gratification. He wants to sense God daily, not just once a week.

SO WHAT'S IT ALL MEAN?

In 1985 the photo print shops were big business, but few photo giants (like Kodak and Polaroid) recognized the coming digital age would effectively end the era of print photography. A digital photo could be cropped, resized, recolored, and, most importantly, easily stored by a person. The middle man was gone. Few people need a processor anymore, especially if they own a computer and printer. We print what we want, when we want. We take endless photos and delete the bad, ugly, or out of focus. The consumer, not a company, is now in control.

Everything has changed. In 2008, Polaroid filed for bankruptcy. The next year, Kodak announced its legendary Kodachrome film was history. Film was obsolete. Paper may be next, as digital photo frames that flash hundreds of photos are more engaging than a single photograph on a wall.

Obsolescence happens. And the smaller church better not overlook its own potential to grow archaic.

"The current church culture in North America is on life support. It is living off the work, money, and energy of previous generations from a previous world order. The plug will be pulled either when the money runs out (80% of money given to congregations comes from people aged fifty-five and older) or when the remaining three-fourths of a generation who are institutional loyalists die off or both."

—Reggie McNeal, missional leader and author *Present Future: Six Tough Questions for the Church*

Here today, gone tomorrow. Like a dot-com company in these new cultural waters, we can soar and sink in seconds. That's why youth ministry in smaller churches begins with socio-cultural exploration and contextual understanding. Reinvention and innovation are treasured tools in the contemporary paradigm. It's why *small is tall*. The larger you are, the harder it is to reinvent and innovate for relevance. Change is shackled to policies and procedures, rules and regulations. Smaller church youth ministries can move fast and free. They can react to change, stop on a dime, turn in an instant, and reroute if necessary. It's no longer 1985.

The future is *now*, but don't live to seize the day. Cultural change happens so quickly you must, in Leonard Sweet's words, learn to "carpe mañana" or seize tomorrow so you're continually reinventing relevance. It's why you should be enthusiastic and excited about limited size. While larger churches scramble to find traction in a changing world, the smaller congregation has a decided edge to surf the cultural waves. We have the possibility and potential to speed up and brake to a stop in seconds. We can embrace opportunity and options in cultural traffic jams that delay larger churches.

We have chances and choices to deepen relationships, initiate experiences, and communicate relevance.

Small *is* tall.

It's no secret the church is always emerging and changing. The irony is it's also constant and the "same yesterday, today, and tomorrow." Smallness allows the church to react with authenticity, simplicity, and veracity. The bane of the church, at any time in its long history, has always been bigness. Not that size is bad (it's not), but with size come problems.

"We are living in a world changing at blinding speed, yet in our homes, churches, and Christian colleges we unconsciously prepare our young to live and serve God in the world in which we grew up instead of in the world of the third millennium… As a consequence of leaders' failing to lead with foresight… we have missed a lot of opportunities to advance the gospel of Christ in a changing world. Instead of driving into the future with our eyes firmly fixed on our rearview mirrors, we need leaders who learn to lead with foresight."

—Tom Sine, futurist and author
Mustard Seed vs. McWorld: Reinventing Life and Faith for the Future

---

Largeness naturally creates the need to organize, categorize, prioritize, and mechanize. The bigger you are, the more robotic you become.

Spontaneity and flexibility—and the ability to change with cultural winds—get lost with tradition, rituals, fear, and sometimes arrogance to not mess with success.

It's why smaller churches and their youth ministries produce a natural spark for change. Megan is a 10th-grader who lives in a small town in western Oregon. She never imagined how a simple act of sacrifice could change her church and community. Convicted by her materialism and closet packed with clothes, Megan held a family yard sale where everything was free to needy parents and their kids. It was a wild success and Megan was hooked on helping the underprivileged. She organized a similar yard sale the following year by marshalling several other families to join the effort and held it at her church. The response was even greater in the town and county. By the fifth year, she was helping more than 200 families in her community with free clothes, household goods, and even food. Who knows where her vision could end?

Every movement starts out small. Jesus changed the world with 12 average Joes. Martin Luther launched a reformation with a single document nailed to the door of a Wittenberg church. Most of the celebrated megachurches in America started small, some in school gyms or living rooms. Imagine the potential that exists in a smaller church where even one person commits to revolution beyond the status quo. Imagine the possibility that's wrapped in a smaller church when a single individual resolves no longer to be ruled by mediocrity, apathy, and small-thinking.

Just imagine. Megan would tell you it changes the world. In the 21st century, small is tall.

My grandmother used to say, "Dynamite comes in small packages." She was right, as there are countless smaller things that have created a tsunami of cultural attention and change.

A cell phone the size of a deck of cards can transmit, publish, film, photograph, text, and connect millions of people. A single e-mail can inform masses, and a solitary unknown can inspire millions. Susan Boyle became a household name in the spring of 2009. This fortyish single English lady lived a rather non-distinct life, until she sang her chops on *Britain's Got Talent*. Even then, it took a YouTube posting of her inspiring audition for Susan Boyle to become a superstar. Small is tall. Overnight.

James wrote how small things like a tongue or a spark or a rudder can change everything. Jesus taught a parable where a miniscule mustard seed can grow into a tree so large the birds find a home. In the kingdom of God, small is tall. A boy's ordinary fish sandwich can feed thousands. A single word can send legions of demons scrambling. A stroke in the sand can cause accusers to run. The two shortest verses in Scripture say it all: Jesus wept (John 11:35) and pray always (1 Thessalonians 5:17).

WELCOME TO THE NEW WORLD

Change is inevitable. In fact, it's necessary. Any living thing that isn't busy changing is busy dying. Stagnation, stalling, and stopping are a prescription for an epitaph.

The good news is the smaller church has a decided advantage in this ever-changing, fluid, accessible, and temporary culture.

Like a motorbike in L.A. traffic we can change lanes, pass cars, and effortlessly (though not always safely) move through the jams.

You may have noticed that I have a preference toward using "smaller" rather than "small" to describe congregations in this book. That's intentional. If you think and act "smaller" you'll realize larger dreams, goals, and even size, but if you consider yourself "small" you'll think and act "small" and that's not only detrimental, it can be disastrous and deadly. "Small" churches are limited, but "smaller" churches possess powerful possibility. "Small" churches are stuck by circumstance, but "smaller" churches are wired for unbelievable opportunity. If a motorcycle acts like a car it'll waste a lot of time and resources stuck in cultural traffic, but when a two-wheeler recognizes its potential and frees itself from the lanes, it'll find its natural size lends itself to speed and success.

This book is about getting you moving.

THE POWER OF "SMALLER"

I believe in the power of being "smaller."

At 5'4" I used to consider myself a "small" person, but now I realize I'm only "smaller" than "taller" people. Yes, my size has limited opportunities. I gave up playing center in basketball in fourth grade and abandoned any hope of reaching the top bookshelf without a ladder. My size also brings prejudices. Small people are not always given the same breaks. I'm sure my size has lost me a few jobs and girlfriends, but that's OK.

I'm actually glad to be smaller, especially when I fly. While others squirm and squeeze their larger frames into the seats for better comfort, I just smile, thankful

I still have plenty of leg room. On smaller commuter planes I don't have to crouch or worry about banging my head on the ceiling. I can sleep just about anywhere in an airport.

Essentially, I came to terms long ago that I'd always be a smaller man in a taller world. *It's who I am.* Consequently, how I approach my "smallness" is everything. I may have limited height, but I possess unlimited vision. I may encounter some obstacles, but I gain many more opportunities. My attitude is not pint-sized or short or vertically challenged. My heart may dwell in a little body but it's not petite in perspective, purpose, desire, or discipline.

Maybe that's why the church is so often described as the body of Christ. Every "body" is different. And, yes, some churches—due to natural situations like community, denomination, or intent—are "smaller." In fact, in the church world, being "smaller" is the norm. You're part of the majority. Consequently any inferiority complexes we harbor are our own doing. If we think we're "small" we'll produce "small" thinking, mediocre programs, and average results.

But if we can be "smaller" and think "bigger" there's no end to what we can accomplish. That's why I believe smaller church youth ministries hold the key to changing attitudes, shifting paradigms, and creating growth. As a youth ministry goes, so goes the church. A great youth program will attract both kids and parents, and no church will experience growth—spiritually or numerically—unless new blood is pumped through the veins.

If you hunger to discover the "tall" in "small" you'll need to refocus and reclaim the power of smaller. It begins with a refusal to let your size direct your present and dictate your future. You hear it all the time.

"Size matters." "Bigger is better." "Do you want to supersize your order?" But in truth, only shallow people judge a person on height. Everyone knows it's what's inside that matters most.

So what's inside you? What's *inside* your smaller church? What's *inside* your youth ministry?

Face it, it's no longer 1985. The world has changed and will continue to change at breakneck speeds. If you're feeling stuck, it's time to stick it in gear and revel in your smaller sports car nature. It's time to switch lanes, take an exit, or make a U-turn. The world doesn't wait for the church.

Rather, I believe it'll be smaller churches that will light the way for tomorrow's church. Being smaller will allow us to live large.

It's already in us. With God, small is tall!

Steph's 2Cents

Hey there, my smaller church youth ministry friends! Stephanie Caro here and my role in this book is the "in the trenches like you" voice. I'm serving in a smaller church myself. Our Sunday worship average is 125 with about 13 youth who are active in some part of our church's outreach.

To me, change seems to come hard to the small church, especially in the technology area. Is it just my imagination or was my church THE last church in America to get its website up? I can count the number of years on one hand since we got voice mail. Imagine the shock and awe when our secretary began emailing the church newsletter instead of buying postage. Typical change dynamics.

But here's a smaller church perspective for you. Did you know?

- The average size church in America is 75 members.

- The average size youth group is 10 percent of a church's regular Sunday attendees.

- The average Sunday morning attendance is 187.

My youth group is small and average! Praise God! No, I'm serious and here's why: If I think "smaller," it makes my ministry fluid and flexible. If I think just "small," I limit my ministry and lessen its might. I don't know about you, but I'll admit it: I've sold my ministry short with statements like, "We can't do that. We're JUST a small church." My bad.

Come on, I bet you've said it, too. Maybe we should make a pact to eliminate phrases like "we can't" and "we're just" from our ministry vocabulary. What if we rephrase our response when we encounter large group ideas? How does this sound? "Since we're a smaller size group, we get to do things a little differently."

Throw in adjectives like intimate, spontaneous, movable, morphing, free, easier, and accessible. You get the idea.

When I think about what Rick has shared in this chapter, I realize that "small IS tall." In my youth ministry lifetime, I've done it all. I've served the 200-plus mega-youth groups and it was fun. But the disadvantage? I could barely keep up with every kid's name much less know their birthdays or pizza preferences. It was great having a budget and fun facility to meet in, but with those things came meetings. Lots of committee meetings! Lots of accountability to go along with the advantages. I'm not knocking accountability, but it's hard to make mid-course corrections. Like moving the Titanic, large church ministry takes lots of smaller "boats" to turn the tide in a different direction.

Now? My calendar has room to get to each student's big game or spring concert. I know who my teenagers are dating and when they break up. There's time to celebrate each member's birthday. I can actually afford to take the group for ice cream cones without taking out a second mortgage. I couldn't say or do that in my larger group settings. Small IS tall, Rick. Thanks for that!

So, here's what I'm thinking: Why don't we journey through the book together? Let's chat back and forth as we read; post your thoughts on my small church youth ministry site at smallchurchyouthministry.com. Write notes in the book's spaces and margins. Make on-the-spot idea application to your calendar. Morph each chapter's thoughts into your group's setting. We can travel this book together; it'll be fun!

Love, Steph

> "When we hear that cultural changes are occurring, our initial reaction may be to try to pinpoint the new problems and then tweak our ministries to fix them. If we don't see younger people coming into our churches today, perhaps we should just add some hip songs to the worship set. Or maybe if we turn the lights down and add some candles, we'll be addressing this 'postmodern thing' and emerging generations will return to our churches. However it's futile to try to fix a surface issue without knowing the cause."
> (Dan Kimball)

> "And no one puts new wine into old wineskins. For the old skins would burst from the pressure, spilling the wine and ruining the skins. New wine is stored in new wineskins so that both are preserved"
> (Matthew 9:17 NLT).

Starbucks Coffee is the epitome of cultural cool.

The hip coffee houses have baptized America in premium coffee, comfortable couches, mood music, and wireless hotspots. Countless imitators have sprouted, but none can match the giant of special roasts. And yet in recent years, Starbucks sales have surprisingly flattened and even declined. Maybe it was due to recession priorities ($3.50 for a cup of Joe is a luxury). Perhaps other competitors were able to create a better coffee experience. Or maybe Starbucks just got a little too big for its pants and lost focus, adding music CDs, espresso machines, and a slew of other products to its repertoire.

Regardless of the reason, Starbucks enthusiastically embraced the problem and sought a calculated return to its cherished values and original DNA. Of course, if you've ever visited the original Starbucks in downtown

Seattle, founded in 1971 near the well-known Pikes Fish Market, you'd understand why. A few years ago, on a family vacation to the Pacific Northwest, we popped in for coffee at Starbucks No. 1. I was mildly shocked at the bohemian, raw flavor in the Seattle store. The original Starbucks sign was more rustic than the brand published elsewhere, and many of the trappings were missing, including the commercialized aspect. No couches. No drive-through service.

None of those amenities mattered, though. The moment you walked in and placed an order for a latte, frap, or espresso, you felt right at home. The baristas were gregarious and conversational, genuinely interested in you. You could tell they enjoyed their work and gave every cup of coffee their own special touch. The shop was alive and soaked with special tradition that evoked pride not pity. A coffee bean pig proudly perched atop the entry while street musicians serenaded on the sidewalk. At Starbucks No. 1 you didn't feel like another coffee customer. You felt like family.

Consequently, it was no surprise that Starbucks announced some changes to its national chain practices. It was time to get back to the coffee. A Starbucks experience started with the bean but ended with the being. Starbucks didn't brew coffee but a warm fuzzy experience. Starbucks didn't sell a cup of piping hot, flavored water but an invitation to connect, congregate, and commune. In some ways, the "drive-through" strategy cheapened the real experience of conversation and friendship created over a cup of coffee. And all the extras—like music sales—only commercialized the experience. People paid big bucks for coffee to relax with a friend, get away from the office, or simply siesta for a few moments. Starbucks was about escape and experience.

"The great difference between present–day Christianity and that of which we read in these [New Testament] letters is that to us it is primarily a performance; to them it was a real experience. We are apt to reduce the Christian religion to a code, or at best a rule of heart and life. To these men it is quite plainly the invasion of their lives by a new quality of life altogether."

—J.B. Phillips, Bible translator and writer (Quoted by Frank Viola in *Reimagining Church*)

And so is the church.

The original DNA of the body of Christ is radically wired for relationship, redemption, and restoration. It's about connection and community. The early church met daily in homes to share meals and stories and learn spiritual truth. It was a safe place for conversation. It was messy at times, too. Relationships are never easy. Ananias and Sapphira lied to Peter (and the Holy Spirit) and dropped dead in their tracks. Eutychus snoozed and fell out the window of a three-story building when the Apostle Paul's preaching ventured past the midnight hour. John Mark had a battle with Paul so severe it cost him a spot on a missionary journey.

Church No. 1 was an engaging, vibrant, frightening community—much different than the 21C version we know today.

A focused youth ministry in a smaller church re-energizes a congregation to reassess and embrace its original DNA format. Youth ministry is never easy, safe, or clean. At its heart, youth work is loaded with emotional danger, soaked with relational dissonance, and immersed in spiritual obstacles. And like Starbucks, sometimes we forget our purpose (relationship, redemption, restoration) and fall prey to gimmicks, fads, and other good but not best strategies.

The problem is when trend becomes tradition and relevance evolves into rut.

Perhaps a historical review would benefit my point.

Consider the church building and in particular your worship "space" (with pulpit, pews, stained glass, baptistery, and piano). Let's be honest, it's the sacred cow and elephant in the room. Church No. 1 didn't have buildings. They met in private homes and gathered in public squares (until driven underground).

"Spirituality is not a formula; it is not a test. It is a relationship. Spirituality is not about competency; it is about intimacy. Spirituality is not about perfection; it is about connection. The way of the spiritual life begins where we are now in the mess of our lives."

—Michael Yaconelli, co-founder of Youth Specialties
Messy Spirituality

For decades the church communed in petite places. In fact, it wasn't until the mid-second century that Christians even built a building for worship experiences, and it wasn't until Constantine's "Christian" reign as Roman emperor that church buildings became the norm (when he sanctioned Christian churches to convert pagan temples into their own gathering places). The earliest Christians didn't go to church. They *were* the church. The place of meeting was immaterial. It wasn't sacred space. Originally, the church was more couch than pew, more conversation than sermon, more food than foyer, and more engaged relationship than passive observance.

Over time, the sacred spaces became tax-exempt temples that literally chained the Bible to the pulpit during the Dark Ages.

During the Middle Ages, the church responded to cultural soundings rooted in emerging technologies like the printing press, telescope, and mechanized clock, to create a passive, systematic, word-based frame. Luther's reformation elevated the sermon, while Calvin's *Institutes* systemized theology. The printing press reproduced the Bible with frightening speed and launched the hymnal to serve the church in worship. The Enlightenment spurred the church into argument and debate—word-rich strategies that appealed to modern ears. Modern education adopted later Industrial Revolution methods that turned learning into an assembly line factory (a format adopted in the church via Sunday school). Church became a building ("we went to church today") not a body ("we are the church") as originally designed.

In the 19th century, an explosion of fresh technologies like the telephone, telegraph, photograph, phonograph, and automobile planted new ideas and communication strategies.

In the 20th century television was invented, and as discussed in the last chapter, it began to shift culture toward moving images and "live" experience. The tipping point for television was two events that occurred within three months of each other: the assassination of John F. Kennedy and the U.S. arrival of the Beatles. Both events galvanized American culture around the television, for news and now entertainment.

Around the same time, innovations in communications were sowing new seeds that would be 20 years or more in the making: cellular phone technology and the World Wide Web. The convergence of these three "mega-techs"—television, cell phone, and Internet—in the late 20th century fueled new communication dialects and, even more importantly, cultural languages. Paper gave way to digital (e-tickets, e-mail, JPEG), aided by wireless and web portals. Connections became more rapid and relationships more wide (Facebook, IM, texting). Visual cues, methods, and strategies reformatted word communication (music videos, PowerPoint, YouTube). Television, in particular, also delivered an experiential component. Video games beckoned players to "get in the game," while reality television reinvented prime time. *Gilligan's Island* morphed into *Survivor*. *Adam 12* and *Chips* turned into *COPS*. *The Love Boat* became *The Bachelor*. It was real people in real situations—or was it?

Why is all this so important to understand? Because if a smaller church youth ministry is going to merge, change lanes, take an exit, or make a U-turn in contemporary culture it'll happen by strategizing through new lenses, namely: *relationships, experiences, and images.*
The smaller church will be ever evolving around the never-changing message of Christ. Reinvention and reproduction are key.

"Television! Teacher, mother, secret lover."

—Homer Simpson, The Simpsons (Quoted at www. quotegarden.com/ television.html)

Television, cell phone, and web technology have spelled an end to modern frames. *The experiential has replaced the passive.* The emerging culture doesn't want to "sit and soak" to understand and engage life—they want to experience it intensely. Today we define our lives by the experiences we collect, some real (fantasy camps, extreme sports) and some fabricated (Wii, Rainforest Café). We also live vicariously through others' experiences (rooting for our favorite *American Idol* or *Amazing Race* contestants). Many of the insights in coming chapters for how smaller church youth ministries can effectively contextualize and communicate truth will employ sensory learning and authentic experiences.

Furthermore, relationship has trumped mechanism. Don't get me wrong—we've always been relational beings, but for a good chunk of the second millennium, humanity basically turned life into a machine. Time was defined in seconds, minutes, and hours. Scripture was recast as chapter and verse. Organization, staff, budgets, and assembly line strategies dominated philosophy and practices in business, education, and even the church. Mechanism, boxes, principles, and frames fueled the modern era. Sermons contained persuasive points. Lessons were reduced to "hook, book, look, and took." Theology was systemized and different interpretations emerged as "modern" denominations. In the process, humanity became a little less "human." We were more rules than relationship, more club than community, more organization than organism. One of the hidden blessings of the new emerging culture is the value upon radical transparency, authenticity, and social communion (Facebook, Twitter, PostSecret).

Finally, image is everything. Words still matter, but only if they are marinated within story, metaphor, or parable. Words now live out loud.

"*Christianity—in a centralized, administrative, bureaucratic form—is certainly irrelevant… we must get rid of the hierarchy [in the Church] if we want participation. But we don't have to wish for it. It's happening.*"

—Marshall McLuhan, professor and communication theorist (Quoted by Shane Hipps in *The Hidden Power of Electronic Culture*)

It's been said that C.S. Lewis strongly resisted (even in some cases resented) attempts to create a visual interpretation (cartoon, movie) of his *Chronicles of Narnia* stories. To Lewis, anyone who even ventured to "visualize" Aslan the lion would fail in the capture. The beauty of Narnia and the countless odd characters were experienced only in the mind's eye. Of course, Lewis probably never imagined digital technology, virtual reality, and computer images so lifelike you'd *think* they were real. But when you consider it, Lewis was right. It's hard to now read the *Narnia* books without feeling a little cheated. If you've seen the *Narnia* movies you know what Aslan looks like—according to Hollywood. That impression is so deep that when we read Lewis' stories now we see Hollywood's "Aslan" rather than the one we originally imagined.

Perhaps all this cultural change is confusing, but it's really rather simple. No matter what you want to accomplish in your smaller church youth ministry (in evangelism, socials, worship, service/mission, and discipleship) just think R-E-I. *Relationships. Experiences. Images.* The emerging younger generations are wired to connect (instantly), experience (deeply), and hear through an image (vividly).

THE MICRO-WAVE

Many futurists predict our cultural frames will continue to splinter and merge into countless "micro" formations. Essentially, small will be tall. It's already happening. Hotel rooms called "pods" are emerging around the globe. These micro-rooms are built for one yet feature most of the amenities of regular accommodations. Have you seen the "Nano" car?

> *"Some people automatically turn to technology for a solution. Others never turn to technology for a solution. Some people draw a line in the sand and reject only new technology. The Amish draw the line at about the year 1900. The Neo-Luddites draw a line at the end of World War II. The Catholic Church took its stand against the pill and abortion in the 1960s and hasn't budged. But most of us have a relationship with technology that rebounds from one extreme to another. One moment we're afraid of it, one moment inspired by its power."*
>
> —John Naisbitt, futurist and author
> *High Tech High Touch: Technology and our Search for Meaning*

It's all the buzz in Europe and originated in Asia. It's a sub-sub compact vehicle that sells for the tiny price of $2,500 in India. The iPod continues to shrink in size, as have cell phones. The age of excess in home buying may also be over, as houses as tiny as a tree house are currying favor.

The church has always been smaller in size. In fact, the megachurch explosion is a mere blip on the church history radar. In Church No. 1, thousands converted to Christianity but gathered in homes by the handful. Similarly, the micro-church, house church, and other small group gatherings (like worship experiences, Bible studies, and coffee house "theology" meetings) are clearly going to grow in popularity in the future, especially in places where persecution and pressure against Christianity continue to rise.

The micro-church is intentionally small as it targets specific ages, interests, ethnicities, and neighborhoods. It's recapturing the original DNA of the church by being missional. Christianity finds life in the mall and marketplace, the crossroads and coliseums. Furthermore, home churches are making a surprising impact, especially in the American context. Micro-churches, home fellowships, and small group Bible studies (not connected to any church program) are gaining favor.

Another trend will be networked and community churches. These are smaller congregations that have linked together to share resources, staff, and facilities. In some places the cell church is quite effective. These are house churches that meet weekly (or more) and then once a month congregate with three to six other house churches—sometimes called a pod—for a larger worship gathering in a school, hotel, or some other rented space.

As pods grow and replicate, they force quarterly and eventually annual meetings in larger venues. Every pod is networked with the others and shares resources, staff, rented facilities, and philosophy.

The micro-church is also finding traction among certain ethnic groups—Asian, Hispanic—who meet in private homes, back rooms, and sometime in off-hours at a local church. Regardless of the type, the rise of smaller congregations—some networked into megachurch movements—will be the face of the church in the coming years.

TRANSFORMING PROBLEMS

I'll never forget my first youth group in a small northeastern Nebraska town. I was newly hired as the "weekend" youth minister for a church of 90. My job was to guide a group of kids into a radical, life-changing, amazing faith with Jesus. Of course, this was back when I was a young man, still in college, and under the impression that I was something "special." I remember promising the search committee that I'd revive their youth group and triple it in a year!

My first Sunday was a baptism in reality.

I showed up to teach Sunday school to the teenagers and quickly learned a "prospect" list of 15 kids was actually 4 in number. The apathy was pretty deep and the superficiality of the faith disappointing. I also discovered youth ministry in the small church had few resources. My budget, after begging for funding, was $10 a week! I learned creative ways to stretch a dollar and live larger than the bottom line. I never did triple that youth group and vowed never again to promise what was God's blessing anyway.

"...a younger generation...is embracing new Web-based tools in a way that often confounds older generations but promises real advantages...Tools such as blogs, wikis, chat rooms, peer-to-peer networks, and personal broadcasting are putting unprecedented power in the hands of individual workers to communicate and collaborate more productively."

—Don Tapscott and Anthony D. Williams
Wikinomics: How Mass Collaboration Changes Everything

However, I did learn countless valuable lessons in working with a few teenagers and children that framed my philosophy of youth work for years to come and still impacts fundamental beliefs to this day.

Lesson No. 1: *Every problem is pregnant with possibility.*

Simply put, it's easy to fall prey to discouragement, disappointment, and depression in smaller church youth ministry. It's hard not to play the comparison game, lathered in self-pity and sprinkled with poor self-worth. The obstacles are often overwhelming, but with God they are not impossible to overcome.

MONEY, MONEY, MONEY

I wish I had a dime every time I desired just one more dime to "do" youth ministry. Money greases the program wheels, and more funding means more outreach. Most youth ministers—regardless of church size—feel the frustration of limited youth ministry budgets. Yet the aggravation intensifies in smaller churches, which may have trouble paying heating bills, let alone budgeting for the latest programming "box" subscription.

A lack of funds cripples a youth ministry. Because the budget is small, many youth groups must raise money for activities. I heard of one smaller church where the youth minister's salary was directly linked to fundraising success! It didn't take long for his focus to be more upon the "Benjamins" than the Bens in his group.

Few smaller churches will ever enjoy a budget like the big boys. This reality creates frustration and discouragement. The challenge, then, is to use limited resources in creative ways.

Maybe an overseas mission trip is beyond possibility, but that doesn't mean you can't connect, engage, and resource missionaries using the Internet. The World Wide Web has brought the world to the church.

It's all in how you look at the problem. In chapter 11 we'll investigate more fully the inadequacy of funding and how to creatively "stretch the dollar."

VOLUNTEER SHORTAGES

I've been there many times. My activity, event, or program is woefully understaffed. The consequences have been severe at times but fortunately not disastrous or tragic. It would take several years of youth ministry for me to discover why volunteers—great ones—would suddenly disappear after my arrival. In my case, I was a classic "lone ranger" youth worker. My youthful energy and enthusiasm, coupled with a drive for perfection, deflated my volunteer staffs. I lost a lot of great workers in those early years, many of which were spent in smaller congregations.

Smaller churches often lament their ability to recruit, retain, and motivate volunteers. Consequently many smaller congregations are constantly in "recruit" mode and prone to understaffed situations.

For example, one of the best practices in Christian education is to employ team-teaching. For the smaller church this seems like an impossible task, but in reality, it's far easier to recruit someone to a team than than a solo effort. In chapter 10 we'll explore great insights and ideas to engage and energize volunteers.

THE NUMBERS GAME

It's a common problem in smaller church youth ministry: low attendance. In a youth group of 20, if a third of the teenagers don't show, that's a big deal. It can change the curriculum, alter the activity, or postpone the party. Many times I've had to change course and correct for paltry numbers.

I once served as a Sunday school teacher for a preteen class in a small Pennsylvania church of 65. One morning I waited a lifetime for no one to come. Well, almost no one. I did have one kid. As the clock ticked closer to class time and we both realized it might just be a twosome for our lesson on King Solomon, I could see nervousness dance in his eyes. Normally we had nearly a dozen but for whatever reason, this time it was just the two of us.

My mind started to race with responses. Cancel the lesson and send him to sit with his parents. Snag a video from the church library and waste an hour. Just talk about life or take a walk in the neighborhood. I definitely knew the curriculum lesson wasn't going to work (how was I going to split into three groups?).

And then an idea popped.

With his parents' permission, we jumped in my car and went to Burger King. I bought the boy breakfast and slapped a BK paper crown on his head as we chatted about Solomon's riches and his fragile (paper) empire. The point was made. Later that week, I got a call from his mom. She phoned to say he was still talking about Sunday's lesson. That's when I realized a powerful point: *Don't count the kids but make the kids count.*

You can't do anything about low numbers. They happen. But whether you've got 10 or 1, be slow to cancel, quick to reinvent, and fast to celebrate and confirm. God may only bring a few to your meeting because he wants to do something special. It's not how many come, but how many change in the end.

BOREDOM AND APATHY

Apathy kills youth groups. It's a cancer that first attaches itself to the attitude of your group and spreads until it controls values and vision. Boredom is the result of predictability. Our minds are wired to absorb new information, and when our environment grows predictable (the same thing over and over) we commence to bore (then snore).

We should never dismiss apathy and boredom in our group, but it's also not to be feared either. In another youth group I served, the boredom and apathy controlled the group. I decided to exploit the obvious and created an "apathy" party. Talk about a dull time. Everything was plain, vanilla, or the same. I read to them from the dictionary—in monotone. We yawned until our stomachs hurt. We ate unsalted crackers and drank water for snacks.

I closed the monotonous meeting with a challenge about apathy and why it was hurting our group. The experience sparked discussion and, to my surprise, changed their outlook. By handing off the problem to my group, they began to own it and the healing process began.

LITTLE TO NO TIME

Smaller churches are packed with generalists, Jacks-of-all-trades, and Jills who wear multiple hats. It's not unusual for your better volunteers to oversee other ministries, handle special duties, or manage various resources. If you're the youth minister the job description can be packed to the gills. Consequently, it's inevitable that time (or the lack thereof) becomes a factor.

After all, time is like money these days, and it seems like it's always a recession.

Larger churches are helped by professional staff (overseeing specific ages), but smaller churches are either volunteer-led or employ a single youth pastor to administrate the nursery, oversee children's church, plan middle school lock-ins, direct VBS, guide Christmas pageants, lead a choir, coordinate mission trips, and supervise a slug of other activities in between.

The key is to remember your priorities and to stop "majoring in minors." Delegate whenever possible. Learn to say no. Carve out significant time to spend with your family. Many ministry marriages teeter due to over-extension, and to paraphrase Jesus: *"What does it profit a youth leader to win a whole high school to the kingdom but discover your own family no longer believes?"*

When you quit doing stuff that another person can do, you'll have time to do the things that truly matter.

DISCONTENTMENT AND COMPARISON

Among the conversation starters at most ministry leadership gatherings is THE question: How many do you have now? What's your attendance? It's the barometer of success. Consequently, comparison and competition are no strangers in smaller church youth work. The "bigger is better" syndrome is easy to adopt, and when natural obstacles rise to discourage our work, it's common to fall prey to discontentment and play the comparison game.

If anyone had reason to be disappointed in the numbers game it was Jesus. Early in his ministry thousands flocked to hear him teach and work miracles, but when his lessons got hard and following Jesus became a difficult choice and sacrifice they dropped out in droves. On the day he was crucified only John witnessed his execution. Judas had betrayed him. Peter denied even knowing him. The rest of his followers were scattered and scared.

In many eyes, Jesus' ministry was a complete failure. Of course, we know the rest of the story. The mission of Christ was not popularity, power, prominence, or prosperity, but service and sacrifice. He chose a ragtag bunch of fishermen, rebels, and IRS agents to change the world. The homeless, the outcast, the possessed, the sick, and the sinful followed Jesus and naturally created complaint, criticism, and condemnation. These days, Jesus probably wouldn't be leading a workshop at a youth ministry convention.

Our disappointments in smaller church youth ministry are often rooted in what we see and hear. And yet, God may be working a greater vision beyond our sight that only time and testing will prove. It's hard to work with an apathetic, troubled, or divisive bunch of teenagers that just don't get it.

> "The power of one has been squared, or even cubed, by mediated culture. No empire is so large it can go it alone; no individual is so small that or she cannot change the world...we are living in a world where very few can kill very many, where even one of us can kill all of us."
>
> —Leonard Sweet, futurist and author
> *The Gospel According to Starbucks*

It's discouraging to experience their lack of commitment in attitude and attendance. It's difficult to stay motivated and easy to accept another opportunity (bigger and better).

But here's a thought: When the grass looks greener on the other side of the fence (and it will), maybe it's time to fertilize and water your own lawn. My hope is that this book will inspire confidence, instill passion, and inform understanding on how to do just that.

I didn't think I was going to jump in mid-chapter but I have to tell ya—all these frustrations existed in my 200-plus youth groups, too. Apathy in abundance and a plethora of 'tude! I remember the summer we unveiled a new bathing suit guideline. At least a third of the girls were ticked! And a third of 100 is a lot bigger pain than a third of 10. More kids sometimes means more visible discouragement. My group now? No matter what we do or who shows up, it's a doable circle of conversation. OK, back to Rick...

CELEBRATING POSSIBILITIES

While smaller churches are ripe with frustration, fears, and failures, they're also packed with unlimited possibilities. Smaller congregations are like an extended family and it's a reunion whenever we gather. There's something special about knowing everyone. The hugs last longer. The handshakes mean more. The smiles seem endless.

Smaller churches also provide greater opportunity for teenagers to be involved. Kids can lead worship, run sound, create PowerPoints, design websites, go on hospital calls with the pastor, pass the offering plate, lead a devotion, and serve as greeters.

In one smaller congregation, during the winter months, teenagers (with driver's licenses) served as parking valets for the elderly or disabled. The young people helped them into the building, parked the vehicles, and returned their cars after services.

The personal touch and opportunity for contact is greater in smaller churches. It's a whole lot easier to connect with 10 kids than 100. You can go to more of their games, recitals, plays, and concerts. The numbers game actually works to your advantage. Even Jesus understood the greatest discipleship happens within smaller contexts (that's why he only chose 12 to be his direct disciples and three to be his inner circle). In many larger congregations, teenagers fall through the cracks and are never missed. They get lost in the crowd. But in the smaller church every face has a place.

Count the kids, you lose. Make the kids count, and you win every time.

My deepest desire is for you to discover the tremendous joy that emerges in working within the smaller church context. No, the problems won't disappear and there'll be plenty of frustration and failure to mark your journey with the teenagers. The key is to embrace with enthusiasm our original DNA. The church is designed for relationship, redemption, and restoration. Smaller churches and their youth ministries possess a powerful potential to unleash those qualities. Size does matter in a changing culture and church landscape, but it's in the seed the tree is defined.

Starbucks figured it out and so must we.

Steph's 2Cents

Wow, chapter two is a lot of brainpower to unpack. A Starbucks white chocolate mocha sounds good about now. Taking a sip...let's dig in. What were your "aha" moments? Here's something I highlighted as I was reading:

"Why is all this so important to understand? Because if a smaller church youth ministry is going to merge, change lanes, take an exit, or make a U-turn in contemporary culture it'll happen by strategizing through new lenses, namely: relationships, experiences, and images. The smaller church will be ever evolving around the never-changing message of Christ. Reinvention and reproduction are key."

"Reinvention and reproduction are key." I'm thinking this would be a good time for us to take an inventory of our churches. What needs reinventing and what should be reproduced? In other words, it's time for a good old-fashioned pro/con list—the ultimate assets/obstacles insight into what we're dealing with in our ministry to youth. (Use the margins of these pages to make your own list.)

My YM Assets:

1. Our church's Coffee Café is a cool pseudo youth room.

2. GREAT projection system for movie nights.

3. I have a large network of youth folks, so I can get cool free stuff.

4. I've been around the YM block a few times. Experience must count for something.

5. Lots of availability and space on the church calendar.

6. Amazing contemporary service that fits our teenagers' worship needs.

7. Students morph well into the life of my church. They'll help with anything just to hang around. Doesn't hurt that I always have food in my office and quarters for soda.

8. I have GREAT kids! (They're making me say this at least twice in the book or I'm not allowed to talk about them.)

My YM Obstacles:

1. NO budget. Zero. Nada.

2. My designated youth hours per week—maybe two? Three tops.

3. Lack of time leads to less of everything: events, recruiting, delegating, and so on.

4. No dedicated space. (But really I'm OK with that. Not a top priority at all.)

5. No staff administrative help.

6. A fair amount of the "good ol' days" denom way of thinking. "The way it used to be."

7. Did I mention there's no youth budget?

I don't know what discoveries you made from your list, but here are two things that surprised me: 1) No big revelation in the obstacles column and 2) I have more assets than I realized! Could I be guilty of focusing on the difficulties of working in a smaller church and not celebrating the huge advantages?

I'm having a light bulb moment. Rick said, "Lesson No. 1: Every problem is pregnant with possibility." When I take a look at my assets list, why don't I do more movie nights at church? Easy, cheap, no prep time, and we can sit on the couches in the café to watch (insert favorite group movie here) on two big screens. (It's awesome; you'll have to trust me on this or come visit.)

My main takeaway from this chapter? Use more of my youth ministry assets to combat my obstacles. Remember my smaller church advantages. Like the movie night idea, I have more at my ministry fingertips than I've been utilizing. There are lots of resources available to show my kids the love of Jesus in the fellowship of his church.

For example: Since I know lots of people in youth ministry, my group and I could invite ourselves to other churches' youth events. We're fun people! Or if my kids like to hang out in my office, why not ask them for admin help? Work off that soda money! And when all else fails? We have lots of rooms to play "glow in the dark manhunt."

CHAPTER THREE  GROWING TALL
WHILE STAYING SMALL

When I was a child, I spoke and thought and reasoned as a child. But when I grew up, I put away childish things (1 Corinthians 13:11 NLT).

Kids grow up fast. My daughter is about to graduate from college, and my son is in high school. It seems only like yesterday they were playing tag in the backyard, learning their ABCs and watching Barney. Now Ryan drives our car and Becca works full time to pay her own bills.

Children are incredibly wonderful. Their passion for life is boundless. They love to laugh, explore, play, and dance. They like to question, and their attention spans are as short as their stature. I think we all know we treat children differently based upon their age. In fact, because babies and toddlers tend to be quite messy and prone to mishap, we overlook their failings with great grace. If a preschooler spills his milk, it usually evokes a different reaction than if a preteen tips the glass.

Consequently, in local church ministry, we understand these differences change how we teach and lead children. We recognize developmental variances and even sometimes exploit them for educational gain. It's easy to bribe a kid with a candy bar or Bible Buck, but such tactics lose their luster with a teenager.

Though candy does have a special power! I know I'll do almost anything for some Reese's at certain points of a youth event. And if you want to really win my heart? White chocolate. My birthday is March 11th; I'm just saying...

Kids who can't read or write are at greater disadvantage when placed in older classes. Expectations grow with age. With age comes size, and with size comes different responsibilities.

Similarly, the size of the church is a lot like human age, except you can be 110 years old and still stuck in a crib wearing a diaper. As with human development, a church grows in size and evolves into a different entity. It may retain similar values, but it'll possess a different mood, a different structure, a different method, and a different power to pursue greater things. Smaller congregations are trapped within child bodies that are limited by size, resources, ability, and opportunity. It's not that we don't want to be "big" but it's simply not possible. We are what we are.

I'm not totally agreeing with you on this one, Rick. I know smaller churches that feel their call is to be more intimate in size, yet still have plenty of opportunity, resources, and abilities. My church, for example. We don't feel trapped. Yes, we are who we are and we're happy with that. God's blessed us with a lot. But maybe before I judge too much, I should read on...

That's why it's a myth that one size fits all. Or one program fits every church. Or one philosophy matches all congregations.

Too many smaller congregations buy into adult (large church) fashions to wear on their diminutive frames.

Like David's failed attempt to wear King Saul's armor to slay Goliath, we end up tripping over our shirt tails, continuously pulling up our over-sized trousers, and trying to do what the big boys and girls claim works for them. But when the program falls flat or the dream never flies, we get discouraged and disillusioned.

Instead of celebrating our differences and enjoying our stature we hunger to be tall or big or "mega." Instead of embracing our childhood we lust for adolescence. Consequently, we grow frustrated, discontent, and sometimes apathetic. David had it right. Ditch the oversized fashions and slay the Goliaths with slings and stones better fit for a boy.

Too often we view size as success when, in truth, it's perfectly acceptable to be a healthy child *forever*. It's OK to be an *eternal* preschooler. If God decides to grow your congregation then that's a different story. However, many smaller churches are small not by intent but by context. Small towns produce smaller churches. Segregated ethnic communities keep congregations naturally tiny. Church age means your size is also limited. Few church plants start off running. Most must toddle and experience the "terrible twos" for a season.

That's why it's important to recognize the differences in the smaller congregation. What if you imagined your church not by age (time) but by developmental difference (numbers)?

- Under 20 active attenders = an infant

- 21-50 active attenders = a toddler

- 51-100 active attenders = a young child

- 101-150 active attenders = a preteen

- 151-200 active attenders = a middle schooler

- 201-350 active attenders = a high schooler

- Over 350 active attenders = an adult

Then Saul gave David his own armor—a bronze helmet and a coat of mail. David put it on, strapped the sword over it, and took a step or two to see what it was like, for he had never worn such things before. "I can't go in these," he protested to Saul. "I'm not used to them." So David took them off again. He picked up five smooth stones from a stream and put them into his shepherd's bag. Then, armed only with his shepherd's staff and sling, he started across the valley to fight the Philistine (1 Samuel 17:38-40 NLT).

"Tipping Points: 150 people"

Malcolm Gladwell, in his insightful book *The Tipping Point: How Little Things Can Make a Big Difference*, notes the magical power of 150 in regards to hierarchies, armies, and even religious groups. He shares how the Hutterites—in the same family as Amish and Mennonites—will form a new colony once they reach 150 people. As one Hutterite explained, "When things get larger than that, people become strangers to one another…in smaller groups people are a lot closer. They're knit together, which is very important if you want to be effective and successful at community life."

A baby church (under 20 in attendance) will act much differently than a preteen church (between 101-150), and a toddler church (between 21-50) has different developmental issues than a middle schooler church (between 151-200). Babies live simpler lives than preteens; and as puberty rearranges the human body, so does surpassing 150 in regular attendance change priorities. The ability to reproduce means a congregation of this size can hire additional staff or build an additional facility. Unfortunately the choices decided as a "middle school" church may stunt any growth that has already occurred or could occur in the future. Countless churches reach adolescence (in numbers) but fail to graduate into adulthood and the middle-sized congregation. Consequently, the majority of all churches in America today are hopelessly a child or teenager in their size.

Anecdotal evidence in my own consultations and study of thousands of American churches suggests if a church hasn't surpassed 350 by its 30th birthday (actual age of congregation) it probably never will. In fact, the greatest high water attendance mark that's reached in those 30 years tends to be the zenith. The DNA of a church is strong by its third decade and usually requires a complete death (property sold, closing) for new growth to sprout. Whatever growth does happen occurs during seasonal moments when attendance swells, usually under a particular pastor's leadership, but only dies on the vine beneath division, conflict, or the pastor's departure. It's rare for a church over 30 years of age to find new life without relocation or major reinvention.

So what does this mean? Simple. Instead of a constant attempt to be "big" (when we're not), we need to embrace our inner "age" (related to our size and not our years as a church) to release potential.

Our inner age frees us to be babies and crawl, depend upon others, and make some messes. Our inner age allows us to think differently as preteens and enjoy new abilities and opportunities that come with growing up. Our inner age unleashes our adolescent angst and lets us clumsily forge a firm identity and purpose for future reproduction in leadership, facilities, and programming.

It's not how old you are (in years) but how young you are (in size) that matters. Different ages mean different reactions. The smaller church varies from larger churches developmentally. We don't have the same body frames, ability to reproduce, skill in programming, and strength in outreach. Like a kid, a smaller church behaves different. And you know what? That's OK!

Church growth expert Lyle Schaller noted in his excellent work *The Small Church is Different!*: "The large church is not an enlarged version of the small congregation, and the small-membership church is not a miniature replica of the big church...They are almost as different from one another as a village is unlike a large central city."[1] Or like a preschooler differs from a middle-aged adult.

Schaller also suggested 20 characteristics unique to the smaller church, but we'll only expand upon eight that are particularly relevant to youth ministry.

THE SMALLER CHURCH IS RELATIONAL

I grew up in a small Montana church of 125 people. We were one big family, and I remain deeply indebted to the saints in that congregation who nurtured my faith through thick and thin. I felt intimately connected, and when my own family disintegrated, I sought sanctuary in

"When the Greeks got the gospel, they turned it into a philosophy; when the Romans got it, they turned it into a government; when the Europeans got it, they turned it into a culture; and when the Americans got it, they turned it into a business."

—Richard Halverson, former chaplain of the U.S. Senate (Quoted by Frank Viola in *Reimagining Church*)

[1] Lyle Schaller, *The Small Church Is Different!* (Nashville, TN: Abingdon Press, 1982), 12-13.

the church for comfort, encouragement, and resources. That little church taught me how to pastor. Most of my jobs came through fellow church members. When I needed a ride, I knew where to go. When I wanted to serve, they had a place for me.

The good news about a smaller church is that everybody knows everybody. The bad news is that everybody does know everybody and, consequently, everybody is seemingly into everybody else's business. Gossip, backbiting, and personal conflicts aren't necessarily lost in larger congregations, but bigger numbers can diffuse their detection.

Larger numbers can also increase the variations of a gossip fest so it's a lose-lose either way, either size. Easier to track down the gossip and correct its effects in a smaller setting.

In the smaller church, the emotional explosions not only split a congregation but can also create serious damage to its reputation in the neighborhood and surrounding community.

This high-relational characteristic is a lot like gasoline. When properly channeled the gas creates the spark for life, ministry, movement, and change but if misfired, it can also ignite a bomb that burns and buries a congregation for years. A smaller church rises and falls on its relationships. The cliques that emerge either welcome or warn guests to move along.

Youth ministries have tremendous power to tear down the relational walls that prevent outsiders from connecting to a congregation. New families are attracted to churches that employ all ages. Smaller congregations flex their relational muscles when they creatively engage visitors.

I know one smaller church that reimburses church members who take new visitors to lunch after services. Another smaller congregation weekly feeds college kids because they have no Sunday meals in their cafeteria.

Relational ministry is incarnational in process. It's outwardly focused in nature (Jesus everywhere in the world). It's constantly creating community that ripples into the neighborhood. Smaller congregations that lose outward focus become highly resistant cliques (Jesus alone in our church). It's fine once you bust in the door, but most people won't go to that emotional effort.

THE SMALLER CHURCH IS TOUGH

If you hang around a smaller church long enough you'll hear the proverb: *"This too shall pass."* At first glance such a statement seems rather depressing, but in reality it's a liberating concept. Smaller congregations have learned to weather many a storm, especially churches that have been around 30 years or more. It's an attitude that sweats toughness. *Been there, done that. We've seen it all before. No worries, stuff happens. We'll survive, we always have.*

Consequently when crisis or conflict rocks a smaller congregation it almost always bounces back. Much of this toughness is rooted in a veracious loyalty to the local body. During one particular season of great discontent in our family's congregation, I encouraged my grandmother to attend a different church in town. Her response was priceless: *"Why? This is my church."* It's this tough, "never say die" attitude that makes the smaller church particularly unique. It won't take no for an answer. It won't shut down until all options are exhausted. It won't quit just because another church in town is doing it better. True of my church!

Smaller churches' natural resilience and deep commitment create a firm context for youth ministry. One time my grandmother, at the tender age of 65, volunteered to lead the youth group when nobody else would. She moved the meetings to her home for the few kids still coming and fed them supper, followed by Bible study. Suddenly the group started to grow. Ten kids. Then 15. Then 25. The group's growth was related to her resolve to not give up on them (and probably the burgers and fries she served).

Smaller churches and their youth ministries are different because they can create a deeper ownership in the community. Not everyone gets to play in the praise band at a bigger church, but there's always room in the smaller congregation. These opportunities instill individual loyalty and create congregational ownership.

THE SMALLER CHURCH IS A VOLUNTEER ORGANIZATION

One of the great differences between a smaller and larger congregation is how fast the smaller church assimilates people into leadership positions. It's not uncommon in large churches for a person to ride the pew many years before finally joining a volunteer staff.

In the smaller church, it's not only necessary to get involved but unless you're older and have served your time, it's highly expected. Consequently, the volunteer staff may be smaller in number but actually tends to be greater in percentage of the overall church when compared to larger congregations.

The volunteer nature of the smaller congregation certainly creates unique problems. It's not uncommon for desperate leaders to recruit any warm body.

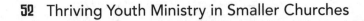

And because the bar is low, so are the expectations to participate in training and comply with policies and standards. Therefore, many smaller church volunteer staffs are woefully underprepared for the work and may produce mediocre results at best. Teachers can be easily seduced into apathy and casual teaching performance. Youth workers can often succumb to shortcuts that impact safety. Sexual predators may operate within churches that relax background checks and prescreening standards to fill a volunteer slot.

OMGosh! Rick, you're reading my mind now and I have to tell you: I don't like it. Without going into details, I ran a check on the ZIP code area around my church for registered sex offenders and found exactly what you're talking about. I realized then that I hadn't done all I should have to protect my church's kids.

Smaller church volunteers also wear multiple hats. I remember one of my youth leaders who also served as the treasurer, an elder, occasional worship leader, Sunday school teacher, and coach for the softball team. No wonder he was mildly stressed! The "cream" in a smaller church usually gets handed a lot of the crop.

Of course, smaller church contexts also have advantages in that volunteers tend to know each other intimately.

Consequently, they're more in tune to personal needs and emotional dynamics that cause a larger staff to disintegrate. Long-time volunteers also know the local resources and can help connect program needs to businesses, schools, government, and other agencies.

Smaller church volunteers may also serve many fruitful years. A small church in Drain, Oregon, boasts a youth ministry that serves missions, significantly impacts the town, and has graduated dozens of kids into Christian leadership.

A major key to its success has been a married couple that led the ministry for three decades! Danny Harrod comments, *"Ray and Roberta never accepted a salary in their 34 years of youth ministry. Neither played a guitar. Neither had a Bible college degree (although Ray is a gifted Bible student and teacher). Neither aspired to be youth workers. They didn't become Christians until their mid-twenties. They learned as they went along."*[2] The church didn't need a paid youth minister. It did better without one. Kids flocked to this volunteer couple for counsel, inspiration, biblical instruction, friendship, and resources.

THE SMALLER CHURCH CARES MORE FOR PEOPLE THAN FOR PERFORMANCE

I'll never forget the time I preached a weekend service for a very small Iowa church in the dead of winter. The church was far from any town, in the middle of nowhere. When I walked in the front door of the large building I was immediately struck by the chill. The unheated sanctuary easily seated a few hundred but it was clearly vacant.

I learned the church was hanging on with only the faithful few, most hailing from two long-time church families who couldn't stand to see the once-great building sold. The small crowd forced everyone to a downstairs fellowship hall where the smell of cinnamon rolls and coffee tempted the senses.

This church's worship was hardly professional. In fact, by most standards, it was atrocious. Kids played with their toys and disrupted the service.

[2]Danny Harrod, *Unleashing the Potential of the Smaller Church*, edited by Shawn McMullen (Cincinnati: Standard Publishing, 2006): 99.

The singing brought new meaning to "make a joyful noise." The steel chairs were uncomfortable and the piano out of tune (featuring an elderly pianist who only played chords).

After the offering and just prior to my message, a 20-something girl stood to sing "Amazing Grace" for us. To say it was awful was an understatement. She didn't hit a single note and literally squawked and squealed. I was stunned by the performance and surprised when the place erupted in wild applause for her effort. She paused, smiled, and then signed "I love you" to her admirers.

Suddenly I understood. The girl was completely deaf (since birth). She sang from her heart the notes as she knew them, and to those with ears to hear she produced an angelic melody. I learned a valuable lesson that day about the beauty of the smaller congregation. It's not about performance but people. It's not about getting it right but just getting it. It's not about hitting the notes but lifting the spirit.

The reason many don't feel like they belong at church is we've swallowed the myth that quality is everything. Now, I'm not saying we shouldn't do things well or excuse mediocrity, but I am saying smaller churches can revel in being messy places where imperfect people find their cause and calling through often sloppy avenues. Mistakes are OK. Stuff happens.

It's why grace is so amazing.

THE SMALLER CHURCH REWARDS GENERALISTS

In a smaller congregation every person plays a part. Sunday's organist can be Monday's office secretary. Wednesday's youth leader can be Saturday's choir director. Tuesday's women's Bible study teacher can be Friday's cook.

In larger churches, volunteers specialize. In smaller churches, volunteers serve widely. Many part-time and weekend youth ministers understand their job doesn't stop with teenagers. Often they lead elementary ministries too, including children's church and VBS. Because of this "generalist" context, a few problems emerge:

- **People get overcommitted.** It's hard to say "no" for those who find personal pleasure and purpose in Christian service.

- **People never develop specialized skills.** If you're leading Sunday worship, teaching Sunday school, and administrating the missions of a church, your interests are varied and can easily be superficial within specialized skill sets.

On the other hand, the generalist nature of smaller churches creates opportunity:

- **People are flexible.** They can fill in at a moment's notice. They can switch classes. They can take on additional roles.

- **People know what's going on in the whole church.** In larger churches, youth ministry tends to become isolated from other programming, but if you have generalist volunteers there's more communication.

People know what's happening in other programs, including scheduling conflicts and interpersonal relationships.

- **People can use their gifts and talents.** Many volunteers are pigeonholed in larger churches through their regular work and reputation. *You're in public relations? Great! You can handle our publicity.* The problem is they may seek and sense God's leading for other types of ministries. Smaller churches allow volunteers to experiment and test different callings.

THE SMALLER CHURCH IS INTERGENERATIONAL

The larger a church becomes, the more age-segregated it gets. The largest of churches silo their ministries beneath professional staff and even separate buildings. It's not uncommon for children to never worship with adults until they graduate from elementary school. I'm currently consulting with one megachurch where the middle school and high school pastors hardly speak to each another—and nobody talks to the children's minister!

Smaller churches are unique in that they exude intergenerational opportunities. Preschoolers feel safe to take candy from a generous senior saint. Teenagers hang out with children. Grandparents openly chide and correct misbehavior beyond their family.

Programs tend to be "all-church" in nature, whether fellowship dinners, ice cream socials, softball games, or retreats.

The consequence of an intergenerational context cannot be understated. Young people are far more involved in church life in the smaller congregation. In one small church I served, I desperately needed adult volunteers for an elementary program, but none stepped to the plate. I then invited my older teenagers to lead the children—handling games, snacks, and even lessons. In a few short months they were even planning outside activities.

One hazard, however, is the inability to focus on pure and specific needs. One church planned a Valentine's party just for its teenagers in order to encourage purity and teach about dating relationships. But as often happens in smaller churches, other groups caught wind of the party and wanted to be involved.

Eventually the event morphed into an "all-church" Valentine meal and the focus upon purity and dating was dropped from the agenda.

THE SMALLER CHURCH HAS A PLACE FOR EVERYONE

Youth ministry naturally attracts all types of kids, but smaller congregations level the playing field and create unique space for adolescents to be known. In teen culture there are many social frames: skaters, punks, nerds, preps, jocks, cheerleaders, computer geeks, and fashion freaks. And like the *Cheers* theme song, teenagers hunger for a place "where everybody knows your name."

Community starts by belonging to something bigger. Our identity is forged and framed by those with whom we associate.

Consequently teenagers may be labeled in larger contexts (school, for example) by their skills, interests, economic status, or race, but in smaller contexts they are finally known more as "Jimmy" and "Juan" and "LaShawna" and "Li." Only within smaller subgroups are we truly known and our names overpower the labels that unleash the true person inside.

Most would think a larger church would also be a place for everyone, but that isn't always true. Many larger youth groups are quite homogenous in nature, attracting a particular slice of teen culture and life. Consequently there are "skater youth groups" and "athlete youth groups" where the majority of kids tend to socialize within similar contexts. As a result, outside kids who can't connect drop out.

Larger church programs have numbers on their side pouring in the front door and, consequently, tend to overlook the back door.

However, in the smaller church youth group, it's hard to exit without being noticed. Even if you attend once and never plan to return, your name is on a roll or mailing list that may linger for months. Yes, smaller youth groups can be cliquish—usually along similar social slices—but teenagers who overcome their fears of association literally unlock a place where every student feels welcome and loved.

THE SMALLER CHURCH FOLLOWS A DIFFERENT CALENDAR

Churches are like locomotives. The larger you get, the more programs (cars) you pull down the track.

If you only have a few it's easy to quickly pick up steam and speed. Of course, if you're pulling dozens of cars the startup is snail-pace slow. It takes several miles to reach maximum speed and also requires more time and track to eventually brake to a full stop.

The larger a church gets, the more time and track are needed to get a program moving or even to kill it. In the smaller church, sheer lack of size allows for sudden track changes, swaps, and exits. Imagine pulling together a rafting trip for 100 kids. The logistics alone reveal my point. You'd have to plan several months in advance how you would transport, feed, and get all those kids safely down the river. You'd also learn quickly that every stop or break would last much longer as you try to keep dozens of kids moving in the same direction. Meals would take more time. Consequently, the potential for boredom (and trouble) is greater. And what happens if a van or bus breaks down? What happens if one kid gets hurt? What happens if weather pauses or postpones the event? Every plan has three backups. By the end of the trip, you're exhausted. It's a lot of work to manage 100 kids. And we haven't even mentioned the publicity, promotion, expense, and advance notice needed to ensure all the logistics succeed.

Now let's say you decide to go river rafting and you want to invite your small youth group of 10 kids to join the fun. Details could be worked out in a couple weeks, even days. You could save money by borrowing a raft, not renting one. Food would be a snap, and a single van would transport the group. A few phone calls, an e-mail blast, and a Facebook invite, and you're all set to raft.

Another dynamic is the political structure that controls a church. In a larger context, the hoops are numerous to secure vans, publicize, and even get the activity on the calendar.

In the smaller church, there are fewer channels, and it's far easier to gain approval for an event.

Of course, the hidden danger to these advantages is actually a failure to plan. Because we can do things quickly and pull off events faster, many smaller church youth leaders play sloppy with details and loose with promotion. Consequently stuff happens that doesn't need to occur. Some parents get miffed because they didn't know about the float trip. The raft you borrowed is missing paddles or there aren't enough life vests.

The greatest error in smaller church youth ministry is a failure to plan properly. It's so convenient to just throw events together that it's easy to miss the benefits of carefully planned meetings and events.

A FINAL WORD...

If you've paid attention to these differences and how they affect youth ministry, then you'd agree they're tremendous advantages. Many times we focus upon the obstacles and miss the opportunities, or we are waylaid by the problems and miss the possibilities.

The secret to effective smaller church youth ministry isn't to walk around in oversized clothing (programs, structures, policies) fit for somebody bigger. Rather it's tapping into our inner child and opening our eyes to see differently. It's recognizing our toughness makes us stronger and seeing how deep community carves purpose.

It's learning to walk, even with an occasional fall, as an intergenerational volunteer organization that thrives on flexibility, spontaneity, fluidity, and personal touches.

Often smaller congregations compare themselves to larger churches and wonder "if only?" but what you may not realize is larger congregations are constantly refining and reorganizing to become "smaller" again. We possess what they readily recognize as the key to continued growth and influence.

When we try to be something we aren't, we steal the joy and hope that's waiting to work in our favor and for our future. The differences light the path for potential and promise. So, yes, smaller churches are different! It's a blessing. Our smallness makes us big in number. Our size makes us large in influence.

It just takes the faith of a child to really see it.

Steph's 2 Cents

Loving these eight points, Rick (and Lyle)! OK, friends, time to unpack our youth ministry suitcases point by point.

The smaller church...

Is Relational:

"A smaller church rises and falls on its relationships." As I chew on this, I'm flipping through my mind's Rolodex. What relationships in my church are a blessing to me and the youth ministry? How are they a blessing? _____
_____
_____
_____

What relationships challenge the success of the youth program? Why? And what can I do about it? _____
_____
_____
_____

Is Tough:

Amen! Three things you can count on: death, taxes, Jesus, and roller coaster rides in smaller churches. Wait—that's four. Some of my church's leaders are going through a "dip in the road" right now. What to do when you find yourself in a touch spot at church? Dress yourself in God's Word and get others to cover you in prayer. Call me; I'll pray for ya.

Is a Volunteer Organization:

I know, recruiting volunteers takes time you and I don't have to be better organized in delegating responsibilities—but your ministry's effectiveness is worse off without taking the time. Write down what you can't or won't do and put together a puzzle of others to help out. I personally don't let people get away with the "I'm too old; I've done my time" excuse.

One abundance in my area of the country is a plethora of older folks with time on their hands looking for significant purpose. I love tapping into their desire to serve and be needed.

Cares More for People than for Performance:

So what if our praise band's piano player is a woman of an unknown age? Or our teenagers never quite get the skit right? And we are for sure NOT the coolest, hippest-looking church in town. There's a lot of room for making the occasional mistake. In other words, "Love covers a multitude of sins."

Rewards Generalists:

Reward or punishment? Depends how you look at it, I guess. Multiple people wearing multiple hats. We have one woman who teaches the preschool Sunday morning class, serves on our personnel committee, and is my partner in creative worship planning.

Is Intergenerational:

I don't know about your church, but mine HAS to be intergenerational because there's not enough of us to go around otherwise. Our VBS is a prime example. It takes all ages to make it happen and everyone just gets involved. It's a big week for my church!

Has a Place for Everyone:

Have you ever watched the classic Christmas cartoon Rudolph the Red-Nosed Reindeer? Remember the "Island of Misfit Toys"? That's my church and I love it! There's no sense of worrying over our image or achieving a certain look. We don't have the time or resources for "image"—nor do we care. We are who we are and we do what we do.

Lots of our folks have different challenges and needs, but everyone seems to find their niche. No one stands out because we're all different. For example, there's our office administrator who has no arms or legs. Single moms with children who look different than they do. A faithful regular who lives in the woods nearby who always wears a hat that says, "My Boss is Jesus." And me. Glad they let me in.

Follows a Different Calendar:

In my days of 200-plus youth groups, nothing moved quickly. To do our kids justice and get the word out, events had to be planned more than 12 months out. We could NEVER just up and change the plan on a whim without the risk of disappointing a lot of kids and leaving them out of the loop. All it takes now are a round of e-mails, a phone call to a student without a computer, and a text to get the word out about something different. With that said, a smaller church youth ministry should still plan six months out in pen, 12 months out in pencil.

"The first Reformation was about freeing the church. The new Reformation is about freeing God's people from the church (the institution).

"The original Reformation decentralized the church. The new Reformation decentralizes ministry...the initial Reformation was about church. The new Reformation is about mission."[1] (Reggie McNeal)

In 21C culture small is the new tall. Miniature is the new giant. You want to be a Goliath? Learn to be a David.

The emergence of the "micro-church" or "mini-church" is the face of the future church. In his critically acclaimed work *Microtrends: Small Forces Behind Tomorrow's Big Changes*, Mark J. Penn wrote:

> the whole idea that there are a few huge trends that determine how America and the world work is breaking down. There are no longer a couple of megaforces sweeping us all along. Instead, America and the world are being pulled apart by an intricate maze of choices, accumulating in 'microtrends'— small, under-the-radar forces that can involve as little as 1 percent of the population, but which are powerfully shaping our society.[2]

Essentially, niche is the new mass. "Microtrends" possess mega-influence and power to reinvent and reorient society. For many futurists the church of tomorrow will look more like a Walgreens than Wal-Mart—small, neighborhood pharmacy-department-grocery stores planted strategically through the suburbs, small towns, and urban centers that target a niche culture.

[1] Reggie McNeal, *The Present Future: Six Tough Questions For Your Church* (San Francisco: Jossey-Bass, 2003): 43.
[2] Mark J. Penn, *Microtrends: The Small Forces Behind Tomorrow's Big Changes* (Twelve, 2007): xii-xii.

Churches will also become more blended in the future, similar to how KFC and A&W operate from the same store or McDonald's and Subway anchor a gas station.

The fastest growing types of congregations are non-denominational, community, or covenant in title. They may be small in size but massive in overall numbers.

Consequently, youth ministry in smaller churches will need to abandon the one-size-fits-all approach and intentionally incarnate (become Jesus) to their specific neighborhoods. If the teenagers that walk the sidewalk outside your church are skaters, then focus upon skater ministry. If the families surrounding your church are primarily Hispanic, then maybe it's time to learn Español! Ironically, Penn outlined the "Hispanic Protestant" as one "microtrend" and the "Mini-churched" as another, noting that currently there are over 10,000 unique global religions today and every day another two or three new ones are added.[3] As Penn concluded, "religion is fractionalizing, and the ability to bring together many people under a single religious banner is dwindling."[4]

In the smaller church there are additional "microtrends" emerging, including increased acceptance and employment of women clergy and greater numbers of pastors without formal seminary training. Many youth workers in the smaller church have little to no biblical education or specialized training in youth ministry.

Another smaller church "microtrend" is the graying professional youth worker.

I know the number of a great hair guy near me that can take care of that "graying" thing for you. I see him every six weeks.

[3] Penn cites the *World Christian Encyclopedia*. Ibid., 312.
[4] Ibid., 314.

The explosion of megachurches and swelling of middle-sized churches in the 1980s and 1990s created a youth pastor shortage in many denominations. Consequently, the mid-sized church has been plucking college graduates (rather than the modestly experienced) in recent years to lead their youth programs. This has left the smaller church with few leftover college résumés and forced many to hire more mature youth workers. Many of these older youth workers are former volunteers, but there's also a growing pool of aging professional youth ministers available. Some of these 35- to 50-something professionals have found it difficult to be hired by larger churches (who prefer the 20-something) and also prefer a return to more personal youth ministry.

This is so true for me; I'm loving it!

What this means is there are four basic types of smaller church youth workers, and each is a "microtrend" in context.

THE VOLUNTEER YOUTH WORKER

Shari is a typical smaller church youth worker. She works as an office assistant 40 hours a week, runs her two teenage boys to various sporting practices and games, cleans house, shops for groceries, and cooks the evening meal. She's also working on her master's degree. Three years ago, her small church of 125 lost its youth minister and in the process of seeking a replacement, Shari stepped up to the plate as a volunteer. As the months passed, then years, she became the primary youth leader for kids who affectionately call her "mom."

Nevertheless, some weeks the hours get long and she feels the pressure to give what she doesn't own: more time. She has to tell a lot of church teenagers "no" or "not this time" or "let's try to do it in the future." Some parents want more out of the youth program, and some of the lessons and events don't get the time they need. Often Shari leaves church feeling discouraged.

Is she really making any difference? Would anyone care if she quit?

The unpaid volunteer is the largest segment of smaller church youth workers. Most congregations are simply too small to hire even a part-time person to lead the youth ministry. Consequently, these churches rely upon volunteers (usually parents) to answer the call and oversee activities, lessons, and youth events. Unfortunately, the expectations upon a volunteer can be high, especially if families leave for other church youth ministries. Most volunteers are gripped by some common frustrations:

- Lack of time to spend with the students

- Lack of personal time for family, hobbies, and outside interests

- Lack of training in youth ministry

- Lack of resources—or wisdom to pick the right resources

- Lack of congregational support and feeling left alone to do the ministry

- Lack of communication with church staff and leadership

The frustrations create a lot pressure on volunteer leaders who won't last unless they are passionately called to the task.

The average volunteer survives less than six months on the job, and most quit because they feel inadequate, unappreciated, and tired.

One possible solution is to avoid the one-youth-worker-leads-all approach altogether. Some smaller churches recruit multiple volunteers to lead the youth ministry, including every spiritually sound parent of a student in the youth program (it's a well-stated expectation of parents). Many hands make light work and multiple volunteers spread the load for effective results. Some parents only lead youth trips (because they own vans). Others only lead worship (because they play an instrument). Still others only teach or counsel or plan or fundraise. Every volunteer has his or her niche. To paraphrase an African proverb: *"It takes a whole church to disciple a kid in the faith."*

The training frustration is easily resolved through social networking (seek out professional youth ministers on Facebook for resources, ideas, and insight), websites, and inexpensive training events. Volunteers will often balk at training events that require time away from home, but these opportunities are invaluable for motivation, encouragement, and instruction. Smaller churches that seriously desire an effective youth program should build into their budgets monies to pay all volunteer expenses to training events.

It's also OK for a volunteer to say "no" or "enough." It's perfectly fine to set limits on your time, resources, and skills. If all you can give is one hour a week, then invest your best into those 60 minutes. Don't be afraid to take a break. If you're burning out, you're effectiveness has already eroded. Some smaller churches purposely schedule no youth programming during August and December so volunteers have time for personal vacations and breathers.

"For centuries, the tour guide metaphor has dominated our religious experience. We've defined evangelism and spiritual leadership in terms of a hierarchical relationship: one person finds the way and tells someone else how to get there. By contrast, the church of the future—the emerging church—would seem to embrace a more collaborative leadership model. The metaphor is that of a traveler— someone who is 'on the way,' journeying with us. They may still have more experience and expertise than we do, but they don't need the security of their position/ title. They can lead a group without having to know absolutely everything about the final destination."

—Spencer Burke, church leader and author *Making Sense of Church: Eavesdropping on Emerging Conversations About God, Community, and Culture*

On the other hand, perhaps you can be more creative with your time and manage it more effectively. Lots of teenagers are currently on Facebook. It's a great place to connect and communicate so develop a presence. You'll learn a lot about what's happening in your students' lives via their status updates, and you'll never miss their birthdays again! You can also send special prayer messages to students, upload devotional thoughts, create a "fan" page for your group, and post photos. It sounds like a lot of work, but if you could give even 15 minutes a day to Facebook youth ministry, you'd see a difference—plus it's a lot of fun! If Facebook no longer exists by the time you read this, then connect to the social media site where the teenagers are hanging out.

Finally, create a strategy for effective communication to your pastor, parents, and kids. E-mail and text messages may be the most obvious choices, but perhaps a phone call is faster and more efficient. Be sure to coordinate all activities and events through your leadership. Some volunteer leaders "feel" abandoned because they fail to communicate. If you want connection, you need to be the plug.

THE PASTOR WITH YOUTH MINISTRY RESPONSIBILITIES

Jason pastors a small church of 45 in southwest Kansas. This 110-year-old church has seen its trials. At one time it was *the* church in town, boasting a large youth group of nearly 80, but changing times and internal struggle have left their mark—and produced a single-digit youth group. Jason's age was partly why he got the job. He's 25, and the church leaders felt he could attract some younger families and connect with teenagers.

Unfortunately, in Jason's brief two-year ministry he's faced mounting criticism—despite growing the youth group to around a dozen. The children's ministry is in disarray, and he can't help it. He also feels inadequate for youth ministry. After all, he majored in preaching at Bible college and had only one course in youth work. He has never felt "called" to youth ministry but does it by default. His mentor, another small church pastor across town, has encouraged him to just let the youth ministry die. "It was the best decision for my ministry," the older minister confided. "I simply couldn't do it all."

That's not an option for Jason. It's an expected part of his job.

It's a common problem for smaller church pastors, especially younger ones who are either pressured to develop youth programming or feel a burden to do something—anything. Many confess it's an enjoyable outlet and they don't mind creating events, going to conferences, or counseling students. For others, however, it's a draining expectation. Older pastors of small churches, in particular, sense frustrating pressures to either recruit a volunteer staff or step aside for someone who can better "relate" to the kids.

Consequently, many smaller church pastors experience:

- Guilt that they should be doing more for the youth

- Apathy to lead a work for which they sense no calling

- Inadequacy and ignorance about contemporary youth ministry trends, resources, and programming

- Lack of support and quality in available volunteers

Smaller church pastors are busy individuals. Many hours can be poured into solo ministry: weddings, funerals, hospital calls, nursing home visitations, sermon preparation, lesson study, counseling, leadership development, cleaning the bathrooms, fixing the copier, typing the bulletin, and planning a retreat (and that's just Monday!). Consequently, a pastor's commitment to youth work is connected to his calling and desires to lead youth.

An additional problem emerges if the church starts to grow and the responsibilities and expectations rise as a result.

Regardless of the situation, pastors must recognize the value of youth ministry and focus upon generating good will and a positive attitude about leading students. In my experience and consultation with small church pastors and church leaders, attitude is the key. In my first youth ministry, I'll never forget my 60-something preacher's desire to accompany the youth group to a Christian rock concert. He was completely out of his element. He wore a suit and tie, sat in the back, and packed his ears with cotton. The music was not to his taste, but he never criticized or complained. He confessed his mission was to understand. When several of the kids shared how this artist's music changed them, he supported their commitments and commended their conviction. In return, he earned the teenagers' affection and allegiance.

Pastors can also use contemporary illustrations and address adolescent concerns in their messages. This is tricky because what seems like yesterday can be years ago. A teenager's frame of reference is about 7-10 years. Simply put, that great movie illustration from 2001 will fall flat with most of them.

A great solution is to meet regularly with a teenager to discuss your messages. One pastor announces his upcoming sermon schedule and encourages his teenagers to send him YouTube links.

Find some time to learn about youth ministry.
Subscribe to Group Magazine or the Youth Leaders Only (music subscription) service. Take a veteran youth minister or ministry professor to lunch and pick their brain. Google "youth ministry" and enjoy a web journey.

Download youth ministry podcasts from iTunes. In today's web culture there's no excuse for being uninformed.

Finally, just be you. Forget all the stereotypes about youth ministers. You don't need to tote a guitar, get a tattoo, shop at Aéropostale, or listen to the latest music to relate to kids. Most teenagers aren't looking for another friend but a trusted mentor who's friendly. Share your gifts and abilities and time. *Like to fish?* Take a teenager to the lake. *Enjoy baseball?* Invite some adolescent fans to join you. *Are you a fan of barbeque?* Host a grilling party. Spend time praying for the youth. Write an encouraging word on their Facebook walls. Let them know you're thinking of them with a call or text message.

THE PART-TIME YOUTH WORKER

Amber is a student minister for a church 70 miles away. During the week she has 18 hours of school, a part-time job, and a fiancé, but every Saturday morning she packs her bags for her weekend youth ministry. Amber enjoys the drive but often arrives tired from a long week of school.

On Saturday it's local ballgames, home visits, and hanging with teenagers, while on Sunday she teaches a Bible lesson, leads children's church, goes to lunch with a church family, rests in the afternoon, and finishes the day with youth group at 5 p.m. She'll be back at school by 9 or 10 p.m., if there are no other meetings.

Amber will confess she's often gone to her ministry sick, because if she stays home she loses pay ($150 plus gas). She needs the money to pay tuition. She'll also admit she doesn't always give her best. Preparation time is limited. She is just learning about youth ministry in her classes and doesn't have many resources. She also gets frustrated at a few parents and church leaders who want more out of her. "I'm giving all I can right now," she confides. "I feel guilty that I can't do more."

In many mid-size smaller churches—from 75 to 150 in attendance—the answer is to hire a part-time intern or weekend youth minister. Of course this option primarily serves congregations near a Christian college with a youth ministry department. Many student youth ministers need places to put hands and feet on their education. I must confess my three weekend ministries and two summer internships were invaluable for me as a student.

But here's the problem with outsourcing your youth ministry: It rarely pays dividends in the end (except to the student). Weekend ministries are only slightly more effective than no youth ministry at all. In fact, a volunteer-only youth ministry is far better than reliance upon a weekend/part-time youth work. Look at this way. If you pay a $175/week salary to a student plus travel expenses, it's easy to spend $800/month or nearly $10,000 a year investing in a student who probably will be gone within two years—some small churches hire a new youth minister every year!

This discontinuity breeds apathy among the teenagers (no consistent leadership) and deflects potential volunteers (that's why we hired a part-timer). It's not uncommon for some church teenagers to experience five or more part-time youth ministers during their adolescent years. What type of message does this send?

Now think of the ministry (resources, event-funding, scholarships) you could purchase with that same $10,000! A church can significantly underwrite a youth program and fund volunteers to attend training and purchase quality resources, curriculum, magazine subscriptions, and equipment. It's infinitely a wiser choice than hiring a part-time youth worker—both practically and economically.

Nevertheless, many churches hire part-time youth workers and these workers have their own frustrations, including:

- The difficulty of balancing school, ministry, and personal life

- The difficulty of youth ministry by proxy or from a distance

- The poor salary compared to similar hours in another job

- The lack of experience and feelings of inadequacy

In my 15 years as a youth ministry professor I helped many students and churches to develop a positive part-time experience. **The key is for both parties to recognize the priorities of the student: God, family, school, and then the church.** This is the primary reason why a weekend ministry is hardly profitable for a local congregation.

For these priorities to work properly, a church has to sacrifice and view its youth ministry as a training ground, rather than a potential program for spiritual and numerical growth. Student ministers are young and inexperienced, prone to make multiple mistakes. Furthermore, when conflict or stress becomes great, they can quit on a moment's notice.

Part-time youth ministry can be effective and moderately successful if several conditions are in place, including a firm commitment to priorities. A student/part-time youth worker is always a student. Many part-timers are church members who also work full-time in another job. The priorities for both types remain the same. First of all, you need a dedicated commitment to growing your own relationship with God. You can't give what you don't own. Second, if you have a spouse and kids, you need to recognize they're your primary youth group. If you're spending more time with church kids than your own, something's wrong. Third, you need to develop healthy relationships with peers your own age. You're not a "big kid," and teenagers can't be your "best friends." The fastest way to burnout and emotional emptiness is draining your life of accountability and community. Fourth, your schooling or work is more important than the church. If youth ministry is crowding your studies or costing you on the job, you need to re-evaluate. Finally, you need to be responsible to yourself. Eat right. Get your sleep. Take sabbaticals. Enjoy a hobby.

Another secret to successful part-time ministry is delegation and support. This is where a church can help a student succeed. Recognize he or she needs help and recruit quality workers to assist in youth ministry. Go to bat for the part-time youth worker and provide breaks. Many churches give their student ministers a paid weekend off prior to final exams.

Other churches give paid vacation and sick time of one week or seven days per year. Still others pay the tuition to encourage school. Of course, many of these strategies create a need for additional youth workers to step up and help.

It's also important to limit expectations. Too many parents can pressure a student minister or part-time youth worker to "do more" or "fix their kid." Pastors and church leaders might need to run interference and temper unrealistic expectations. A part-timer can't participate in every church function, program, or meeting. Consequently, many congregations use job descriptions to ease expectations and clearly communicate what truly is expected.

THE FULL-TIME YOUTH WORKER

Scott helped plant a church in his Texas community 10 years ago and recently was hired to serve as the church's first paid youth minister. His background is in marketing, and he's served from the beginning as a well-respected volunteer. Nevertheless it's a different world doing full-time youth ministry in this growing congregation of 225. His youth group now numbers near 70, and he's been given additional responsibilities in overseeing the children's ministry. Last week, to his surprise, he had a job offer to jump to a larger church with a salary closer to what he was making in the marketing world.

If anything frustrates Scott it's the higher expectations. When he was a volunteer leader the staff and parents recognized his limited involvement, but now that he's full-time those expectations have greatly increased. He also feels alone (a few of his volunteers even quit when he was hired).

He doesn't know any other youth ministers, but desperately wants to make some connections.

The full-time youth minister in a smaller church is a rarity. In order to financially support a full-timer in the long-term, it means the congregation is pushing 200 and if further growth continues, the congregation may move beyond small church definition. Nevertheless, the full-time youth worker is not without frustrations:

- A lower salary than same-age peers in professional youth ministry

- Multiple responsibilities beyond just teenagers

- Higher expectations due to full-time paid status

- A tendency to feel isolated and unaware of youth worker fellowships

- A feeling that success comes in moving up to a larger church

Naturally, the journey as a full-time youth worker begins in the embrace of professional standards and practices. As with any job, if salary and benefits are an issue or there are temptations to leave for another position, it requires tact and communication. Money is rarely the solution, but tragically in many smaller congregations the only way to get a raise is to change jobs. Just realize that every dollar has an expectation. Sometimes less is better.

It's also crucial to develop a plan to juggle various responsibilities. You'll probably never specialize, but that doesn't mean you can't be effective and successful. You may even discover you enjoy small group or children's ministry. You also can't change expectations, but you can help your congregation to appreciate your unique personality and gifts.

If expectations become harsh, extreme, or unrealistic, seek the counsel of your pastor or church board.

Be careful about initiating too much change too fast. Smaller congregations tend to resist change, especially wholesale changes that alter the fabric of the community. Unless you've been hired from within the church, it's best to let time become your friend. Here are few tips for starting right:

- Time your arrival carefully. July or August is a great starter month.

- Make some "noise." Ask to lead a Bible study, give announcements, serve at a ladies' function, lead a committee, or even preach.

- Succeed early. Create a sure-fire winner event that will attract attention and appreciation. Do something big that makes people in the congregation glad they hired you.

- Be positive. Support the previous youth leader. Avoid any negative talk. Encourage and edify whenever possible. Use discretion and patience, especially if the previous situation was bad. Get to know your pastor and his family, church leaders and their families, parents, kids, and volunteers. Spend time just listening for their expectations, dreams, frustrations, and fears.

You may also need to adjust your lifestyle, especially if you're moving from the city to a rural small town (or vice versa). I remember how life changed drastically for my family in a move from suburban St. Louis to rural eastern Kentucky. It took several months, even years, to fully appreciate the small town community and Appalachian culture. To help me acclimate I bought a motorcycle, rode with several locals, and explored my beautiful new backyard.

Finally, continuously tap into your gifts and calling.
Know yourself and what you want in life. If you're
successful at all, other churches will come knocking,
but it may not be a great fit. I've learned, when faced
with various "good" opportunities, to seek God's will
by asking him to actually "close" the door if it's not for
me. I've heard a lot of slamming over the years and felt
great disappointment, but in time I realized God was
protecting me from worse fates.

"Microtrends" not only impact 21C culture but also
how youth ministries are led within the smaller church.
If you sense heat or feel like you've got a target on your
back, it's OK. Whether you're a volunteer or paid—part
time or full time—the secret to survival and success is
a continual focus upon your calling. God has placed
you in this position for a reason. You *know* it's true. Like
Jonah, you may have tried to ditch the call, but it's still
working you over.

The beauty of the smaller congregation is its messiness.
You can actually make a few mistakes in your journey as
a youth worker. You'll park the van in the wrong space.
You'll make a parent mad. You'll spill a lot of liquid on
the church carpet. You may even have a few church rules
named after *you*. There's a church in Ohio that forbids
hiding in the baptistery when playing "Sardines" and
another in Idaho that outlaws tape on the wall. And, yes,
I'm the reason.

They're known as "Because of Rick" rules. In my passion
and enthusiasm for youth ministry, I forgot something
or overlooked a rule—or was plain ignorant. Somebody
was upset and someone else made a new guideline. It
happens. But I don't regret any of my failures or faults.
Those "rules" made me a better youth worker. In every
one of those situations I learned a valuable insight
and gained incredible experience.

In my failures, I have succeeded.

And you will, too.

Steph's 2Cents

So what's my story? Where do I fit in with Rick's list of youth worker types in small churches? I thought you might be wondering because I know I'm wondering who you are.

I think I started in youth ministry in the last part of the 1970s (Go ahead: Roll your eyes. I'm old. Whatever.) The reason the exact date is unknown is because I wasn't really paying attention; I was in before I knew it.

Someone needed to step up and teach the confirmation class of our small little church, and since I was a preacher's kid, I was "voluntold." I must say, I think it went pretty well. I enjoyed doing it, and the students seemed to like it, too.

Can you guess what happened next? The leaders of that church asked if my husband and I would be the youth leaders. After all, we were young so we must know something, right? Apparently, being 20, a preacher's kid, and breathing were the only requirements necessary. So we said yes—suckers.

It went on from there. I thought I was just killing time until a real job came along where I'd make beaucoup bucks in the music/business world. The first job at that church was for free. Was I surprised when another church offered to pay me to lead the youth program. Wow! Working at a church! It would be like walking among angels every day in the office. I figured we'd stop and do Bible study every morning, pray over every little decision. It was going to be a perfect working world!

I can hear you laughing from here. Was I wrong! Of course, that's not how it went at all. I discovered church politics and territories and board rules and how spilling soda in the Ladies Parlor is the unpardonable sin. But I stuck it out in the youth ministry thing. God wouldn't let me out.

I did what a lot of youth workers do. I sort of moved "up" in the ranks of size and salary. I finally arrived at the point where I was serving in a large church and making a living my family could actually live on.

After acquiring a few years under my belt, my youth ministry horizons expanded into writing, speaking, and training—all while still serving in the large church setting.

By the way, the large church also has it proportional share of politics, turf wars, sacred cows.

And "Because of Stephanie" rules like "no manhunt anywhere near the organ pipes."

Thirty years have come and gone. Where am I now? Still serving in the local church but back to part-time in a smaller setting due to traveling so much. I have multiple responsibilities in my role at this church. So, my youth ministry outreach has to be creative. Since I'm on the road a lot, my youth kids have begun to ask if we're meeting in person for our Wednesday night small group study or "will it be on Facebook?" (Which has worked out really cool, btw.)

My ministry with them is a little "catch as catch can" so I involve them in the other stuff I'm doing around the church. I think we're all glad just to spend time together. They help me set up the band, decorate at holidays, open/close up the church, lead VBS, and so on. We definitely don't do enough special events, and I need to work on recruiting parents for that. But we are happy hanging with each other, and friends seem to weave their way in nicely. Proof that kids care more about relationships than they do programming.

(I will admit to spending a small fortune in taking the gang to Starbucks.)

Why am I still in the local church? First, I believe God has called each of us to use our gifts in serving where we worship. Why am I still on staff if even part-time? I want to stay fresh in what I teach and write. Besides, I still love ministry to and with teenagers. Though the color of my roots has changed, my love for shharing Jesus with students hasn't.

But more importantly, I'd like to hear your story. Seriously. Help me make our journey together the best it can be, meeting our smaller church youth ministry needs. Post on smallchurchyouthministry.com or write me at: theemqueen@aol.com. I'd love to hear from you.

Let's get to know the real story about each other.

CHAPTER FIVE  DING! YOU'RE NOW FREE TO MOVE ABOUT THE KINGDOM

I wrote this chapter in seat 12F en route to Phoenix for a reason. It's the first time in a long time that I've actually enjoyed a flight. Over the past decade I've logged hundreds of thousands of miles in domestic flights from Anchorage to Atlanta and Boise to Boston. Flying is a necessary nemesis to what I do, and because I fly just under the radar of first-class status, I'm a coach guy. Naturally, I have my favored airlines—especially those with satellite television, more legroom, and a better snack. And yet none of those amenities matter when I'm delayed, stuck, or stranded.

I just want to get *going*.

That's why I'm smiling right now.

I'm flying the number one airline for quick turnarounds and on-time departures: Southwest Airlines. It's part of the company's unique formula for success for more than three decades. Of course, Southwest wasn't always an aviation giant. At first, it was a small regional airline that initially served Texans with a few targeted flights out of Dallas' Love Field. But today it's a top-five national airline servicing more than 65 cities and millions of loyal passengers.

[1]Kevin & Jackie Freiberg, *Nuts! Southwest Airlines' Crazy Recipe for Business and Personal Success* (New York: Bard Press, 1996): 15.

Southwest Airlines is about fun, friendships, and freedom (*"Ding! You're now free to move around the country"*) and getting people safely from point A to point B on time.

Trust me, that is no easy task in this post-9/11 flight economy.

And yet here I am, waiting for my drink from a perky flight attendant who can't stop smiling and seems genuinely interested in the passengers. I'm not smashed against the window due to a third person in the middle seat. There's no elite first class. No assigned seats. People board and deplane quickly. Turnaround time is usually less than 15 minutes. Of course, it's no-frills flying. No movies, music, snack boxes, or cheesy instruction videos. Nevertheless, Southwest employees clearly enjoy their jobs. They converse with passengers with almost pastoral savvy. Our flight received a pre-takeoff parody of "Heartbreak Hotel" to announce we were cleared to fly—hardly professional, but people in the cabin wildly cheered and felt more relaxed. And I was smiling.

In her insightful leadership book *The Southwest Airlines Way,* Jody Hoffer Gittell explains why this tiny Texan airline has grown to beat the big boys in air transportation. At the heart is a simple motivational mantra that every pilot, gate agent, operations staff, baggage handler, and flight attendant learns: *"Our planes don't make any money sitting on the ground—we have to get them back into the air."*[2]

Essentially, Southwest exists to fly people to their destinations.

Of course every airline would agree—even argue—that's its goal, too, but what makes Southwest radically different?

[2]Jody Hoffer Gittell, *The Southwest Airlines Way* (New York: McGraw-Hill, 2005): 6.

Why is flying Southwest such a positive experience?

And what insights can smaller church youth ministries learn from the ways an insignificant regional airline radically influenced and changed air travel?

The first lesson is to be *different*. Southwest breaks nearly all the rules in air transportation. The company uses point-to-point flying rather than the "hub and spoke" approach. When you fly Southwest it's more like a bus trip. You travel from city to city picking up and dropping off passengers until it's your turn to get off or grab a different flight plan. It's actually more expensive to use this strategy, but when you can turn planes around in 15 minutes (drop, load, and go) you can process more people and turn a profit. When a plane sits, it loses money. Smaller church youth ministries are also different. You can experiment with alternative strategies and choose variant paths for programming.

A second lesson is to focus on *one thing*. Southwest uses only one type of jet: the Boeing 737. While other airline fleets feature everything from petite props to jumbo jets, Southwest can quickly service any plane (and repair if necessary) at any airport. I once waited on one airline for two hours while an inconsequential part was flown from Chicago to St. Louis! Not only did that inconvenience dampen my enthusiasm to travel with this airline again, but it also cost me time and money. Southwest is built on getting people there on time. Similarly, smaller church youth ministries can focus upon a single point of attraction. Maybe it's a sports ministry or a worship experience or a mission trip. *Do something, do it different, and do it well.*

Another lesson is the company's focus upon *high-performance relationships*. At Southwest everyone works together to get a plane back in the air. It's teamwork built on mutual respect.

> *"Of course we can… Most of us had no idea that we couldn't do this, so we just did it."*
>
> —Jody Hoffer Gittell, author
> *The Southwest Airlines Way*

> *"No carrier knows its niche as well as Southwest… People at Southwest don't have to convene a meeting of the sages just to get something done."*
>
> —Jody Hoffer Gittell, author
> *The Southwest Airlines Way*

As one customer service agent said, "No one takes the job of another person for granted. The skycap is just as critical as the pilot. You can always count on the next guy standing there. No one department is any more important than another."[3]

Southwest is also a plucky airline in that it even allowed cameras to spend three seasons documenting its daily world in the riveting reality program *Airline* on A&E. Of course, television isn't interested with the millions who fly Southwest hassle-free and happy. Audiences want to see the fights, fusses, and frustrations. Nevertheless, *Airline* wasn't afraid to show Southwest's worst moments. Just don't miss the deeper point if you ever catch an episode: Every show crisis is calmed because of high-performing relationships that rely upon mutual respect and shared knowledge. Whatever the issue, problem, or concern, Southwest works as a team to make it right and solve the situation.

Smaller church youth ministries must recognize that relational leadership is rooted in mutual respect and shared knowledge. No single person has the answer. We all need to know how to teach, lead a game, or counsel a kid. We all work together to set up, tear down, clean, and drive. No job is more important than another.

My flight with Southwest reminds me how important a positive experience makes a powerful difference. The flight crew's enthusiasm was contagious. Even with a gate delay at arrival, my plane pulled in on time. As I deplaned, the flight attendant thanked me because I confided Southwest is my "favorite" airline. It was a genuine mutual affection. I got my money's worth. Southwest got my business.

[3]Ibid., 34.

Smaller church youth ministries thrive or wilt on how teenagers, parents, church leaders, neighbors, and the community experience your ministry and work. A reputation is earned one person at a time. It can also be lost in a heartbeat.

So what's the secret to creating a positive youth ministry within the smaller church? How can we develop a culture that keeps teenagers and families coming back? What inner forces and needs can we feed to unleash productivity in volunteers, attendance in programming, and confidence in our vision?

FEED THE NEED!

My stomach is rumbling. I'm hungry and deep inside it's saying, "feed me!" The growls from our bellies are like a flag. They remind us to eat. Similarly, inside every person are six inner needs that rumble for attention. When we massage these needs they attract, encourage, connect, empower, protect, and satisfy. In secular psychology they're known as *intrinsic* needs. Abraham Maslow identified five primary levels: physiological, safety, love/belonging, esteem, and self-actualization.[4] In *Control Theory*, William Glasser suggested a similar yet different set of five inner needs: survival, belonging, power, freedom, and fun.[5]

When these intrinsic aren't being fed, a person can experience such results as apathy, insecurity, helplessness, negativity, and boredom. Many smaller churches often experience such feelings and factors without understanding the underlying rumblings that initiated them.

[4]http://en.wikipedia.org/wiki/Maslow%27s_hierarchy_of_needs
[5]http://changeminds.org/explanations/needs/glasser_five_needs.htm

Even worse, some of the tactics, strategies, and ideas many churches use to motivate behavior—even if well-intentioned—can backfire because they bark at these inner needs but can't take a bite.

Nevertheless, while Glasser and Maslow's theories may help us understand intrinsic motivation, they fail to address the deepest human need for spiritual release through mercy and grace. As a smaller church youth ministry, we create a positive and powerful culture, similar to Southwest Airlines, when we invest in feeding the inner needs of kids, parents, volunteers, and leaders. Essentially, we need to feed the G-R-O-W-L-S—six intrinsic needs that motivate positive feelings and behavior. It's how Southwest became a leading airline and it's how you can unleash your youth ministry to truly fly!

GRACE

The deepest spiritual need is the hunger for peace, mercy, and unconditional acceptance and approval. Grace is easy to talk but hard to walk. Grace doesn't point the finger or fix blame but willingly sacrifices and serves, even at personal cost of time, ability, and reputation. At Southwest Airlines supervisors are no better than the frontline personnel, as a few different employees share:

A supervisor fills in spots when people are on breaks, or when we are short on a zone…when agents see the supervisor working consistently, they give more in a crunch. Also, you get respect by working with them.[6]

If there's a delay, supervisors find out what happened. We get ideas on how to do it better next time.

[6]Jody Hoffer Gittell, *The Southwest Airlines Way* (New York: McGraw-Hill, 2005):

If you've got that kind of relationship then they're not going to be afraid.[7]

Even when you did something wrong, they'll ask what happened. You know you screwed up. They'll tell you what you can do so it doesn't happen again. You walk away so upbeat that you work even harder.[8]

And while Southwest Airlines does incorporate some incentives (like $5 meal coupons, gold stars, and recognition plaques), employees are encouraged to look for more than just financial or material gain. The satisfaction of pleasing the flying public, turning a plane around in 15 minutes, resolving a difficult crisis, or working as an airline family is worth more than any prize.

Counter this approach with how many churches—including smaller congregations—attempt to motivate their teenagers: gimmicks and even greed. In over a quarter century of youth ministry I've seen it all (and done a few myself):

- "I'll shave my head if you raise $200 in offering."

- "Bring the most friends next week and you'll win an iPod."

- "Perfect attendance is the only way you'll earn a scholarship for the mission trip."

- "If we can get 50 kids for this trip, I'll buy everyone a conference T-shirt."

- (insert your own here) If you _____ I will _____.

The problem with many of these gimmicks is they promote self-centered behavior and works-righteousness.

[7]Ibid., 74.
[8]Ibid., 75.

What do I get out of doing this for you? It rubs against a "grace-full" culture that allows failure and fault, mishap and mistake. Often we employ incentives to externally motivate behavior—even good and righteous activity—because it works miracles at the time but soon learn it backfires for the long run. What you win 'em with is what you keep 'em with.

Unfortunately, the gimmicks lose their luster (especially to the losers) and you have to keep upping the prize to draw similar results next time. It's the drug of choice for many youth ministries, but it's a dangerous way to manufacture a "high."

Smaller church youth ministries should also be messy places, yet too often, we miss the opportunity to welcome and befriend teenagers "as they are." Cliques naturally fracture community, and in the smaller church it can become one big clique. You're either in or you're out. A positive youth ministry will create space for every type of teenager. It'll forgive, overlook, and tolerate.

Jerry is the kind of kid that rubs people the wrong way. He has an attitude and can easily complain and criticize. Socially, he's a misfit at school and in town. His hair is rarely combed; he's short, pudgy, and struggles to make friends. His lower-middle class family is a disaster. A few years earlier his mother abandoned him and his siblings. His father is abusive and aloof. Jerry lives with his grandparents and seeks solace in dark "devil" music. He's greatly misunderstood by teachers, labeled as a "C" student with no future. Some nights he cries himself to sleep. He feels alone, abandoned, and anxious.

I know Jerry very well because he's "me" back in ninth grade. I was (and am) "Jerry."

Thankfully, I had a smaller church that didn't give up on me when everyone else in my life did. That's grace, my friends. My deepest need was to be accepted without condition, to be loved without strings, to be understood without prejudice. My story is rooted in a small church youth group that tolerated my angst and anger, forgave my faults and failings (including wearing plaid pants and corduroy!), and loved me through times when I preferred death to life. My youth leaders patiently waited and cared, even when I didn't. My closest friends were in the church, and many of them tolerated my bitterness and rage. Ultimately, I was allowed to be "me" and was gently taught how to live and love again.

That's grace. No wonder it's so *amazing*.

RELATIONSHIP

At Southwest Airlines there's a heart in the middle of their logo. It reflects the company's headquarters at Love Field in Dallas, but it's also a reminder that connection and community are the pulse of this airline. Everyone is family and belongs beneath a banner of "shared knowledge, shared goals, and mutual respect."[9]

[9]Ibid., 29.

One Southwest customer service supervisor comments, "The main thing is that everybody cares. We work in so many different areas but it doesn't matter. It's true from the top to the last one hired...Sometimes my friends ask me, why do you like to work at Southwest? I feel like a dork, but it's because everybody cares."[10]

Or as a Southwest pilot noted, "We're predisposed to liking each other...it's mutual respect."[11] I observed this camaraderie when I flew Southwest. As I sat at an empty gate waiting for my flight, I overheard several Southwest employees sharing deeply about their lives. When I finally turned around, I realized the conversation included a captain, service representative, and a gate agent. They were like a family and it showed.

The great advantage (and disadvantage) in smaller church youth ministry is our relational culture. Our size unleashes a power to promote deeper sharing and richer caring. The smallness of our numbers allows for kids to truly connect and commune. It's also our greatest disadvantage, too. We live in a "crowd" culture that loves to "feel" the mass. Consequently, smallness means vulnerability and transparency. You can't wear a mask in a small town, small church, or small youth group. It's why we naturally enjoy the opportunity to meld with the masses and assimilate as we choose.

Perhaps this explains why the tipping point for smaller churches arrives around 150 people. New blood can be threatening. New people might change us. They might create new problems. Once a church grows beyond 150, it morphs into new dimensions. In the larger church there are multiple "smaller" contexts that emerge. No one knows everyone, but there's safety in connecting with a few faithful friends.

[10]Ibid., 30.
[11]Ibid., 35.

What helps a larger church is there are more relational opportunities to provide connection.

In a smaller congregation, there might only be one or two subgroups—three at best. In many smaller churches the youth ministry itself is a powerful subgroup.

Nevertheless, the search to belong is key to powerful and positive youth ministry. A kid has to feel connection, conversation, and community. After all, if you don't belong, it's so long! The difficulty is creating a vibrant culture of community. Many smaller churches feel they're very "friendly" and they are—just to each other! This is where the smaller church youth ministry faces a challenge—maintaining an environment of connection for the existing teenagers and the new kids. Vibrant community seeks expansion and growth. It hungers for new blood to transfuse change and provide fresh perspective.

One smaller church youth worker went to her high school and offered $20 to an unchurched student to come to her youth group. The teenager took the challenge and found the experience miserable on several fronts. Part of the deal (for the money) was to share openly how he felt and what he would suggest for improvement. It turned out to be a good investment. The youth leader challenged her kids, and things truly changed. So much so the unchurched teenager eventually was invited (by another teenager) to make a return visit.

This time he was openly welcomed and accepted. He became a regular attender as a result.

OWNERSHIP

The key component to Southwest's success in flight actually happens on the ground. Every employee has a role and a shared interest in getting planes back into the air. Consequently, despite different roles and responsibilities, no one person is more important than another. It's not unusual for pilots to be seen loading cargo, flight attendants sweeping the cabin for garbage, or for ramp crew to help get a plane loaded.

The goal is to turn around a plane in 15 minutes. That takes a shared team approach. Everyone has a job, but if something happens to slow down an area, then others can assist.

As one Southwest pilot said, "When you come in [to the gate] and see everybody there ready to work, it makes you feel great."[12] This "shared knowledge" is what keeps Southwest flights on time and in the air.

Or as another pilot explained, "Everyone knows exactly what to do...Each part has a great relationship with the rest...There are no great secrets. Every part is just as important as the rest...Everyone knows what everyone else is doing."[13]

This team approach is what makes Southwest successful, and it's a vital ingredient to a positive and powerful youth ministry. In the smaller church, our size naturally lends itself to a team strategy, but unfortunately in many situations it's dysfunctional and even delusional in nature. Just like larger churches, we can fall prey to the "silo" mentality where we separate age groups (children from teenagers, middle school from high school) and fracture team-centered leadership for a solitary "benevolent dictator" strategy.

[12]Ibid., 31.
[13]Ibid., 32.

It's not that these approaches are wrong, but they can be less effective than a holistic team culture.

In many larger congregations, for example, it's not unusual for whole ministries to be disconnected. Consequently, families are fractured when events and activities coincide. In the smaller church that may not happen (or shouldn't), but nevertheless we may "silo" our youth ministries in other ways. One small church tested every teenager's biblical knowledge, and those who passed were given special status—including a free trip to Israel with the pastor. It decimated unity and created a deadly apathy.

In my own early experiences as a youth leader in the smaller church I routinely "silo-ed" my volunteer staff by marginalizing them from the kids. I recruited them to help but preferred to do it myself.

Consequently, I lost a lot of willing, quality workers. I was that "benevolent dictator," too, but soon learned my staff wilted under my expectations and exhortations.

Ownership is a deep human need. Every person hungers to control his or her situation and make a positive contribution. When we dismiss ideas and insights—whether from a teenager, parent, volunteer, or leader—we steal that person's sense of desire to make a difference. When we stifle teenagers and adults from using their God-given talents, abilities, and skills, we rob their sense of responsibility to the community. Suddenly "our" job becomes "my" job. And if you feel like you're left holding the leadership bag alone, there's a reason. If you wonder why teenagers don't want to be involved, there's an answer. They don't possess the power to control and contribute.

WORTH

If ownership is the key to driving a positive youth ministry, then worth is the gasoline. One without the other leaves you stalled.

At Southwest Airlines there's an intentional investment in appreciation and affection that generates goodwill and self-worth. You're not only on the Southwest team (ownership) but you matter to the team (worth). You're special. You're unique. You're wanted. This type of culture starts at the top. Colleen Barrett, president emeritus of Southwest Airlines, is routinely singled out for her innate ability to make employees feel good.

As one employee said, "Colleen remembers everyone and everything—if you have a birthday you'll get a card from her."[14]

Southwest founder Herb Kelleher says, "We try to allow our people to be themselves and not have to surrender their personality when they arrive at Southwest."[15]

Consequently, part of Southwest's appeal and affection is its quirkiness. Employees in costume. Flight attendants who sing flight instructions or do comedy routines. It's also communicated to the customer. When you fly Southwest you feel valued. First of all, because you know they're doing all they can to turn that plane around in 15 minutes. Second, because it's not unusual to hold real conversations with flight attendants. I've seen them actually sit down with a person and talk for a few moments. Kids and families feel valued. Southwest was among the first to allow early boarding for families. And the company's new strategy to attract the business flyer is paying off. Sure, there's no first class amenity, but special boarding privileges and online check-in have reduced the "cattle call" feel of former days.

[14]Ibid., 58.
[15]Ibid., 116.

Smaller church youth ministries can truly launch a powerful and positive work through celebrating uniqueness and affirming worth. It's not that hard to do. Many teenagers are starving for someone to simply encourage them. Volunteers sometimes quit because they feel a lack of purpose. In the smaller church we possess the incredible opportunity to uniquely affirm people and to let them know they are valued.

Feeding this deep need for worth also means dream-casting. A community that values one another also creates vision. It's how I became a writer. My Sunday school teacher one day noted my joy in creative writing. I loved to pen stories and songs. She not only provided opportunity for me to share my odes to joy (ownership), but also encouraged me to consider writing as a career. Of course, I wanted to be a baseball player back then. Writing was fun, but it was not my dream! Nevertheless she planted a seed in my heart.

She saw what I couldn't envision.

Ultimately, your youth ministry flies high on confidence. When you value teenagers, volunteers, families, and leaders, you launch God's work into flight. If you think about it, an airplane shouldn't fly. It's tons of steel that gravity plummets to the ground. But when shaped properly into special design (worth), it flies—and can become a useful tool for humanity.

LAUGHTER

When it comes to a culture of smiles, Southwest busts a gut. From cheesy in-flight songs to khaki shorts and Halloween costumes, it's a company that refuses to take itself too seriously.

It's part of living the "Southwest Way," and the company's website tells prospective employees that they will need a "fun-LUVing attitude" that maintains perspective/balance, celebrates successes, enjoys the work, and is passionately committed to the team.

As one gate agent shared, "We sing and laugh and play games. Let everyone enjoy their job so they'll work and make the company profitable, and give the customer what they want at the same time."[16]

Another station manager adds, "You have to laugh. Weather affects everything, and puts things beyond your control. We always ask people in an evaluation if they are having fun in their job. If they are, there's a good chance they are doing well."[17]

It's no wonder open positions are few and far between at Southwest Airlines. When you're having fun, people want to join your cause—and don't want to leave!

If there is anything *fundamental* to positive youth ministry, especially in the smaller church, it's tickling a person's need to laugh, smile, chuckle, and giggle. You might argue *serious* youth ministry only happens when you're having fun. It's on that raft trip or in that van when kids let loose and real ministry erupts. It's during moments of laughter the tears can well, as guarded secrets are finally shared and masks totally removed. It's when a kid smiles that you sense connection.

Am I saying youth ministry shouldn't be dead serious at times? Not at all. But even Jesus' ministry was soaked in moments of mirth. Some of his greatest miracles happened with a smile, a celebration, or a party. Turning water into wine or feeding thousands of people. It was fun to follow Jesus.

[16]Ibid., 116.
[17]Ibid., 117.

He said funny things like jamming a camel through a needle's eye. He angered the status quo and wasn't afraid to slay sacred cows and heal on the Sabbath. Jesus was unpredictable, gregarious, and a hoot to hang around.

Sure there were times when Jesus got dead serious. He talked tough and watched disciples drop like flies. He wasn't afraid to call it straight, even if it offended his own family.

Southwest can't control the weather, so smile. You can't control a last-minute school band rehearsal that robs your retreat of five teenagers, so chuckle. You can't control emotional baggage that weighs a student's life down, so learn to laugh.

Smaller church youth ministries should be packed with puns, inside jokes, and gut-busting guffaws. When you know all the teenagers—their past, their pain, and their peculiarities—there's plenty of comedic material. Obviously, you don't want your humor to go too far and cause pain to a teenager's self-esteem or sense of worth, but a youth group that laughs together loves together and lives together. A smile energizes a tired and tortured soul, so baptize your students in fun. In one western Kansas youth ministry we had a summer tradition called "Night Fights." It was plain silliness but in this farming community of 2,000 it was beautiful release. All we did was stand in mucky mud and throw strange stuff at each other—things like water balloons, chocolate pudding, chicken soup and eggs—but it worked. The fire department then hosed us off.

It's a memory that still makes me smile.

SAFETY/SECURITY

Since 9/11 the airline business has struggled. The experience of flying has become a lot less fun. Because terrorists targeted airplanes and exploited transportation security, the focus of the fight has been frontline. Consequently, getting through security can be a nightmare. I'm a "three-binner" myself, meaning I have to use three bins to avoid the possibility of extended search. The laptop goes in one bin, the video projector in another, and my wallet, iPod, cellphone, shoes, and plastic bag packed with small liquids round out the third. My roll-on luggage and laptop case complete the ensemble, which resembles a train in the end.

And then there are pre-flight instructions to prepare you for every possible scenario. Some airlines show video, with instructions in multiple languages. And then there are the countless regulations and rules—no smoking in the lavatory, no electronic equipment in use below 10,000 feet, and no lines for the bathroom. Keep your seat belt on and your cell phone off.

Of course, I'm thankful for security measures that guard my life. In flight there are countless hazards, from birds to thunderstorms to turbulence. Seat belts keep us secure. The rules keep us safe. The problem is when one incident leads to a whole new set of rules. Why must we remove our shoes for security? It's because of the "shoe bomber" Richard Reid, who attempted to bring down a plane with a bomb in his sneakers. Yes, rules are a good thing, but who hasn't bristled when a flight attendant chides you for breaking some rule? Flying isn't fun. These days it's on par with pulling out your toenails with pliers.

At Southwest Airlines they get it. Naturally, rules and regulations matter, but the normal, boring pre-flight instructions are brief, relevant, and vital. Most people don't need a lecture on how to buckle a seat belt, and who needs to know every little problem that could occur. If you're not flying over water, why talk about a water landing? It's too much information.

The same thing can happen on the ground, as one Southwest executive explained: "You can get to the point where you saturate yourselves with information, and you get paralyzed…Maintenance could come up with 50 categories of flight delays, if they wanted to. But you end up chasing your tail."[18]

Chasing your tail is a common sport in many youth ministries. We load our programs with rules, regulations, guidelines, and policies (usually in reaction to an incident or a complaint). No food in the foyer. No headphones on the van. No leaving during worship. Some of these rules exist to produce better cooperation and community, but many are merely power plays to satisfy our own control.

Nonetheless, smaller church youth ministries need to be safe and secure environments. If anything, we tend to let down our guard too much. We fail to protect dignity or provide structure. We plan too quickly and overlook hazards in plain view. Sexual predators target smaller churches because they're easy access. No background checks. No references. No training procedures. No problem. The ease in which we can plan an event lends itself to danger. We don't think about why a teenager should never drive other students for a church activity. We just need the extra wheels and figure we'll "get by" this time. And yet it only takes one tragic moment to change everything.

[18]Ibid., 139.

Youth ministry in the smaller church is also ripe for emotional insecurity. Since the numbers are low and everybody knows everybody, it's common to poke fun at someone's expense. We figure students understand when we tease about Claire's offbeat clothes or joke about John's lack of height. They know we love them. Unfortunately such jesting jabs back when teenagers take pot shots at your portly waistline or receding hairline—or more seriously, when the jokes cut away at a teenager's self-esteem and sense of worth.

Positive youth ministry will feed the need for safety and security. We can't expect hungry students to devour a lesson on Lamentations or for sleepy kids to not slumber through our speaking. If the van is too stuffy or too chilly, teenagers will complain. If adolescents don't feel emotionally safe they'll stay away. So consequently sometimes we feed their need with real food, time to rest, attention to details, and affection for their emotional baggage.

The amazing ascent of Southwest Airlines is a modern business miracle. Since 1971, this company has served the public with simple core values, including the "warrior spirit" (hard work, pursuit of excellence, courage, urgency, perseverance, and innovation) and a "servant's heart" (mutual respect, self-sacrifice, and proactive service). We may see Southwest today and marvel at its influence, but we can't forget that the company didn't rise in a minute. Most of its growth has been in the last two decades. It spent the first 20 years setting the system to feed the intrinsic needs and become an attractive, positive, and influential airline. It focused its future through grace, relationship, ownership, worth, laughter, and safety/security.

Southwest Airlines stands as testament that Davids still knock off Goliaths and mustard seeds can still grow to the sky. It's a company that smaller churches, in particular, can emulate. It starts by recognizing that teenagers—like airline customers—are people, too. They're not dogs that we can train to our own design. Positive youth ministry, especially in the smaller church, happens when we invest in people not policies, relationships not rules, and community not commandments.

Ding! You're now free to move about the kingdom!

Steph's 2 Cents

I like the flying analogy, Rick. I fly a lot and still haven't tired of it. I'm a Delta girl myself so it's an unusual travel day that doesn't include a stop in Atlanta. Anyway, friends, let's build on Rick's airplane illustration to take a look at whether our youth ministries are "soaring" or are "at a ground stop due to bad weather."

Grace:
Yes, even on a crowded airplane. Last week, I saw a 6'5" guy switch his aisle seat for the dreaded middle spot so that a non-English speaking mom and 9-year-old daughter could sit next to each other rather than four rows apart. He showed grace by giving up what he didn't have to for someone else's good.

Let's check that with our groups. When grace is needed, is it there? Are students and adults willing to sacrifice? When students mess up, is there love in the place? Truthfully, every group can get better. So how do we improve the "grace temperature among passengers?"

Here's a great lesson on Grace in a Group:

1. Give everyone a 6"-10" blank "paper person" and a pen. On one side, have kids write lots of great details about themselves. Let the students "introduce" their paper people to the group.

2. Have the group read and talk about Ephesians 4:29–32. What grace guidelines can the group glean out of this passage?

3. Have students turn their paper people over and write hurtful things that have been said to them. Invite students to share what they wrote.

4. Ask your students to rip up their paper people. Then each can pass the paper-person-pieces to the teenager on the right.

5. Have each person try to tape back together their friend's paper person and have everyone show the results. Ask how this activity was like/unlike what happens when we're ripped apart in a group by a lack of grace.

Relationships

Relationships begin at the beginning. So, think back to a day when you were at the doorway about to step into a "first-time visit." Maybe it was a new school, new church, new job. Now put yourself into the shoes of your group's first-timers. What does a new student to your group experience?

In a not-so-welcoming environment, it might look something like this:

- Unspoken but still assigned seating on the couches

- Rules for who gets served what when

- One person who seems to pilot every decision and direction

- No one at the door to point them where they need to go

- Economy service for some, first class for others

I don't know what's true for your group but think about it. What would make for a great first-time experience? Here's a short checklist:

- A student-leader is assigned to greet everyone at the door

- A poster or sign at the entrance tells everyone where the evening is headed

- Seating is equal for all, like in a circle of chairs

- Guests are always served first at dinner/snack time

- Someone personally gives each visitor a tour of what's what and where

- An adult is at the door when students depart to leave a lasting good impression

Ownership

Isn't it easier sometimes just to do things ourselves? When we're already stretched thin by wearing too many hats and having not enough hours, it seems quicker to get stuff done rather than delegate ministry tasks to other adults, much less students!

But think about the flight crew on a plane. At least two people keep your plane on track. One or two people greet you at the door. There are more in the back of the plane ready to help you get settled in.

Someone gives the announcements while another grills the people sitting in the exit rows. Everyone helps serve drinks and pretzels, everyone helps pick up your garbage. No one does nothing.

You might not get your Diet Coke if one person did it all. Same for your youth program. No one wants one person to do it, no one can do it all, and no one will last doing it all. Autopilot only works for so long.

To get you started in giving over ownership, here are some ideas on dividing responsibilities:

1. One person to set up chairs for the night

2. One or two people to provide and set up snacks

3. One person to greet at the door and another to say goodbye

4. One to take attendance and pass out flyers, forms, and so on

5. Two to set up and lead a game

6. One to pray; maybe keep an ongoing group prayer journal

7. Two people to clean up, turn off the a/c, and shut down the systems

8. One person to keep up with the website; another with the Facebook page

9. One person to pass around the "we missed you" postcards for signatures

10. Fill in here whatever you never seem to be able to do

Enough said 'cause you get the idea.

Worth

Adult leaders—showing worth to our students begins with us. Equal treatment, time, and tenderness must abound. Don't remember one student's birthday—remember them all. Never show favoritism. Don't leave anyone out in getting last-minute news communicated. Refrain from even slightly cutting humor (believe me this can be a STRUGGLE). Listen first rather than judge. Jesus died for each of us, even for that "on your last nerve" teenager. Even for you.

Laughter

You know how to make it fun. Just do it. If you don't, maybe you should rethink your ministry calling.

Safety

For physical safety, child protection is mandatory in many churches and denominations anyway, so get your plan in place. Now let's talk about emotional safety.

I have a young friend in youth ministry whom I've been coaching. Two or three times a year, I drop in to her youth program to see how it's going. She serves in an economically suppressed rural area and many of her church's families are struggling through life. Her group has attracted a REALLY diverse bunch of kids. Yet everyone fits in. There's a sense of emotional safety, and I've never once heard anyone cut each other down for how they look or dress. It's just not tolerated. Period. Good thing 'cause this group is the only Jesus many of her kids see.

I want the same for my kids. Don't you?

CHAPTER SIX ◎ FISH STICKS!

"Being a part of this little fish market community and experiencing what you see here has made a big difference in my life. I won't bore you with the personal details, but my life was a real mess when I took this job. Working here has literally saved my life. It may sound a little sappy, but I believe I have an obligation to seek out and find ways to demonstrate my gratitude for this life I enjoy...I really believe you can find some of your answers here."
—An employee at Seattle's World Famous Pike Place Fish Market[1]

Jesus called out to them, "Come, follow me, and I will show you how to fish for people!" (Matthew 4:19 NLT).

No trip to Seattle is complete without a tour to the Space Needle and the downtown Pike Place Market. Anchoring these quirky retail shops is the World Famous Pike Place Fish Market, founded in 1930. It's a true fish tale in reinvention and turnaround success. After all, this small shop operated for 56 years in relative obscurity and nearly went bankrupt in 1986. It was a local destination alone, rarely attracting tourists. Furthermore, as larger fishing businesses saturated Seattle, Pike Place Fish Market stalled to near extinction.

The story of transformation began when John Yokoyama, a former employee, purchased the fish market in the mid-1960s. After watching his business wilt and nearly die by the '80s, Yokoyama consulted with a business coach to re-envision his fish market. That's when Yokoyama made a bold commitment to become "world famous." Anybody can hope for such a feat but as the business' website reveals, they accomplished this status "not by spending any money on advertising...but by being truly great with people."[2]

"We want to give each person the experience of having been served and appreciated, whether they buy fish or not. We love them."

—www.pikeplacefish.com/philosophy.html

[1]Stephen C. Lundin, et. al. *Fish!* (New York: Hyperion, 2000), 33.
[2]http://www.pikeplacefish.com/philosophy.html

The secret to Pike Place Fish Market is intentional interaction with everyone who draws near their business and a targeted focus on making a difference in each person's life.

The culture and climate of Pike Place Fish Market is wildly contagious, engaging, and friendly. John Yokoyama explains,

> *For us it means going beyond just providing outstanding service to people. It means really being present with people and relating to them as human beings. You know, stepping outside the usual "we're in business and you're a customer" way of relating to people and intentionally being with them right now, in the present moment, person to person. We take all our attention off ourselves to be only with them...looking for ways to serve them. We're out to discover how we can make their day.*[3]

I LOVE Pike Place and it doesn't hurt that it's across from the original Starbucks, either. No brilliant point here—just wanted to share.

In a sense, Yokoyama and the Pike Place Fish Market employees are evangelists. Yes, they exist to sell seafood, but on an even deeper level, they seek to change the world, one happy customer at a time.

[3]http://www.pikeplacefish.com/About-Us-3.html

Management guru John Christensen was so impressed by the market he compiled four "simple, interconnected practices" to map its meteoric success:[4]

- **Be There** is about being emotionally present for people. It's a compelling message to increase communication and intensify relationships through mutual respect.

- **Play** plugs into a person's creativity and enthusiasm and feeds the need to have fun. It's a spiritual element that coaxes the inquisitive mind to "play" with an insight or idea.

Which is why I love it—fun!

- **Make Their Day** is a deliberate and intentional daily focus to serve and finding simple ways to serve or amuse people to create meaningful memories. It's not viewing someone as a "sale" or a "project" for personal gain but adding value to a life because that's the type of individual you hunger to become.

- **Choose Your Attitude** involves personal responsibility about your mood and daily choices in matters of the heart. It's handling whatever life throws at you and seeking a way to impact people through your choices.

These four premises would make an awesome mission statement for my church...hmmmm.

The success of Pike Place Fish Market didn't happen overnight. It took time to cultivate a climate of presence, play, positive performance, and production. But ask anyone who's been there—it's an engaging place that invites you to catch a fish (even if it's a fake), chat about life, and purchase Dungeness crab or smoked salmon.

[4]http://www.charthouse.com/content.aspx?nodeid=22610

For the diehards there are T-shirts, books, video/photo posts, and a live webcam.

Pike Place Fish Market reveals how "small can be tall" and how resurrections aren't limited to the Bible. It's also a perfect glimpse in how to converse, connect, and cultivate evangelism within a smaller church youth ministry.

SPIRITUAL AND RELIGIOUS

Sharing your faith and creating evangelistic spirit is difficult, especially in a 21C culture that's highly resistant to "church" (though quite open to "spirituality"). Today's teenagers search for meaningful connection and conversation on spiritual matters but are growing increasingly bored with what they find at church. It's not that they oppose Christianity, but they have grown weary of institutional religion. In his 2005 groundbreaking book *Soul Searching: The Religious and Spiritual Lives of America's Teenagers*, Christian Smith outlined several major conclusions about teenagers in the United States, based upon an exhaustive study and personal interviews:

- The vast majority of U.S. teenagers identify themselves as Christian and few appear to dabble in alternative faiths.

- Most U.S. adolescents tend to mimic their parents' faith.

- A substantial minority of U.S. teenagers consistently and regularly practices their faith. About 4 in 10 attend religious services weekly.

- Most U.S. teenagers profess to be theists and believe in divine judgment, but one-third confesses a disbelief in a personal God who's involved in a person's life.

- Religious youth groups are central to spiritual experiences, but less than 40 percent of teenagers claim any involvement. Larger percentages do attend Sunday school once a month, go to a youth conference, or participate in a mission trip.

- Most U.S. teenagers admit their closest friends do not share their religious convictions and say their schools are openly hostile to teenagers that are seriously religious.[5]

Smith identified three types of teenagers from his study: spiritual seekers, the disengaged, and the religiously devoted. He also discovered that while most U.S. adolescents agree that religious claims are valid, most "appear to take a fairly inclusive and pluralistic position about the truth [of] different religions."[6] Essentially, today's teenagers are syncretistic (Don't feel bad; I had to look it up, too—it means the melding of different beliefs) and experimental. If Zen Buddhism enhances their prayer life, they'll adopt it. If yoga makes them feel better, they'll practice it. The teenagers most open to spiritual searches are those from minority religions like Judaism and Mormonism. Protestant teenagers are the least open.

Among the non-religious teenagers, Smith found few atheists and agnostics but did note such adolescents tended to be older, had fewer friends that were religious, and came from homes that put less emphasis upon religious lifestyles, with divorced and disengaged parents.

[5]Christian Smith, with Melinda Lundquist Denton, *Soul Searching: The Religious and Spiritual Lives of American Teenagers* (New York: Oxford University Press, 1985), 68-70.
[6]Ibid., 74.

They also were vulnerable to more negative influences and participated less frequently in organized activities.[7]

The good news is there's a great mass of teenagers seeking God today, but the bad news is many are finding few answers through organized religion and the institution of the contemporary church.

The problem with that scenario is adolescent faith will mature and morph into non-faith or non-religiosity in the ensuing young adult years. It's a well-documented fact that emerging generations are choosing to leave the church with an attitude.

David Kinnaman's conclusion in *unChristian: What a Generation Really Thinks About Christianity* is troubling: *"We have become famous for what we oppose, rather than who we are for."*[8] In a sense, we have traveled the opposite path to infamy as the Pike Place Fish Market. The perception of Christians and Christianity is largely negative among younger generations, especially those recently graduated from high school. Dan Kimball was even more insightful in his work, *They Like Jesus but Not the Church*, outlining several characteristics of how emerging generations view the church:[9]

- The church is an organized religion with a political agenda

- The church is judgmental and negative

- The church is dominated by males and oppresses females

- The church is homophobic

[7]Ibid., 91.
[8]David Kinnaman, *unChristian: What a Generation Really Thinks About Christianity* (Grand Rapids: Baker Books, 2007), 26.
[9]Dan Kimball, *They Like Jesus but Not The Church* (Grand Rapids: Zondervan, 2007), 73-209.

- The church arrogantly claims all other religions are wrong

- The church is full of fundamentalists who take the whole Bible literally

Admittedly, this negativity is an impression helped by Hollywood and primetime television, but many Christians would also agree the church can be a harsh place, with its fair share of hypocrites, oppression, and political machinery. And as the saying goes, first impressions can be lasting ones (even if they're false).

Consequently, the act of evangelism or sharing your faith often begins by absorbing and dissolving personal bias, prejudice, and perception. It's hard enough for any type of church, but the smaller church faces additional obstacles already mentioned—lower attendance, apathy, fewer volunteers, and facility issues.

It also has to overcome negative reactions to natural cliques that can prevent assimilation.

It's nothing new, however. Opposition to God's message is as old as Adam.

Even Jesus wasn't immune to prejudice against his message. He had to counter common ideas about how a rabbi worked. He routinely angered the religious establishment, broke institutional traditions, and operated outside the prejudices of culture. He shattered prejudice by touching a leper, speaking to a Samaritan woman, and entering into Gentile territory like the Decapolis. At every point Jesus faced opposition because his presence alone was unwelcome and his message—even if attractive—was difficult to follow.

As a smaller church youth ministry, evangelism starts with recognition that not every adolescent wants what you have.

Many are quite jaded by cultural authority and institutional hypocrisy. Consequently, if you truly desire to share God's message with teenagers you have to lose some of the baggage most of us learned long ago in church, Bible college, or evangelism courses. In a 21C culture, evangelism looks and feels different. In truth, you must enthusiastically embrace an incarnational, missional approach in order to engage the unchurched, disinterested, agnostic, and religiously resistant teenagers that surround you every day.

What's that mean? For starters, you must start by confessing ecclesiastical bankruptcy. Like the Pike Place Fish Market in 1986, you need a "come to Jesus" moment that admits a need to do things differently to engage today's teenagers—especially those without any vested interest in church stuff. You need a concerted and intentional reorientation and reinvention as a faith community. Every adolescent is an evangelist.

Every one of your teenagers has someone with whom they can share their faith story. The smaller church advantage is its relational edge. Evangelism is nothing more than inviting neighbors to the family table.

It's about life on life.

BECOMING INCARNATIONAL

Incarnation may sound like an introverted flower, but it's actually a deep theological idea that is unique to Christianity. It's what makes Jesus extraordinary and God "God." One of Jesus' names is "Emmanuel," which means "God with us"—and that's *incarnation*. When God, through the person of Jesus Christ, left the beauty and blessing of his heavenly home to park three decades in our neck of the woods, he "incarnated" into our world. The amazing insight is how God arrived on the planet. Jesus didn't show up like Santa Claus from some celestial North Pole packing presents and riding a reindeer-drawn chariot. Jesus didn't appear as a political ruler, marketing expert, or cultural celebrity. He wasn't even born into a royal religious family.

No, God started the human journey with sweat, blood, tears, chills, apprehension, and fear. In a celestial extreme home makeover, God left splendor for splinters, glory for gloom, and divinity for dependence. In order to understand and save humanity, God became human.

Jesus was born in a setting full of dirty, smelly livestock to a pair of parents running with a reputation (unplanned pregnancy, rumors of divorce). Jesus' baby book included visitors like shepherds and eastern astrologers, akin to a nursery call by a gang of used car salesmen and psychics—not exactly high society.

And when news of his birth reached the political powers, Jesus and his family high-tailed it out of town to avoid certain death. From the beginning God knew what it was like to be hated, pigeonholed, labeled, and threatened (a feeling to which most teenagers can relate).

The ministry of Jesus was also all about incarnation: God *with* humanity. Jesus hung out with whores, rebels, and demoniacs. He touched the diseased, spoke to the disenfranchised, and smelled like fish, sawdust, and dirt. Nevertheless, Jesus wasn't socially marginalized. Unlike many religious leaders, he was equally at home with the desperately poor and the insanely rich. He dined in the home of both Pharisee and tax collector. He could command attention in a synagogue, by a boat, or on a hillside.

"...When I ask students from non-Christian homes what brought them into relationships with Jesus, the top responses involve community. Whether they're invited to youth group by a believing friend, or stumbling into Christian community on their own, most students I ask confirm...that relationships with others serve as a precursor to a relationship with God."

—Kara Powell, seminary professor and author (Quoted by *Tony Jones* in *Postmodern Youth Ministry*)

Many of his followers were women and children, two of the most abused, misunderstood, and enslaved people group in first-century culture. Jesus was eventually crucified a criminal but laid to rest in a rich man's tomb. Do you see the picture? Nobody was too holy or horrendous for Jesus.

Everybody mattered. Evangelism starts by being incarnational. It's not just feeling sorry for the pain, it's taking it on personally. It's getting emotionally and physically involved with teenagers' lives, even when they refuse, resist, and rail against you.

Unfortunately, many Christians—regardless of church size—purposely forget our faults and check our crimes at the door. Nobody needs to see our bloody scars and scrapes. Of course, the smaller the church, the less likely you can hide your hurts. It's difficult to don masks to deflect our humanity because they're more easily detected and discovered. Authentic relationships are central to any community, and in the smaller congregation they are far more pronounced.

Corey was the type of kid easily lost in a larger youth group. He enjoyed life on the fringe and cultivated few friendships. He was a loner and liked slipping in (and out) of a situation without detection. He'd arrive late and leave early. And then one day his friend Ryan invited him to his house to play Monopoly. When he arrived, there were a few other teenagers, all from Ryan's church, who immediately greeted him. Corey told his mother he'd probably only be gone a couple hours but was surprised to see the time fly as he struck new conversations and relationships with Ryan's friends. Corey wasn't a church-going kid and wasn't interested in attending religious services, but he was impressed with his newfound buddies.

Unlike other social circles, they didn't judge his jet-black hair, tattoos, piercings, and torn jeans. They seemed genuinely interested in him as a person: his hobbies, his history, and his home life. When the party finally broke up, Corey was invited by Jake to join them the next week at his house for movies and popcorn.

Within six months, Corey was an active member of the smaller congregation—all because of Monopoly and movies, not at the church or some programmed event, but in a neighborhood home on a Friday night.

Incarnational ministry is rooted in seeing kids as God sees kids. We get a glimpse of Jesus' heart when he confessed the crowds were like wandering sheep, helpless and harassed. Sounds a lot like today's teen culture, doesn't it?

For many of us within smaller church youth ministry we depend upon evangelistic technique and strategy—often counter-relational—to share our faith. We teach the teenagers to memorize principles, laws, arguments, and Scripture verses (all of which are not necessarily bad) but get discouraged when kids rarely "evangelize." In fact, many churches—large or small—have grooved their congregations to be anti-evangelistic. Let the pastor seal the deal, perform the baptism, take the confession, or lead the prayer. Or we create "evangelistic" outreaches for teenagers to bring their friends to "hear" the gospel (which tend to resemble a classic "bait and switch" sales approach). Or we just hand out some tracts. Evangelism, for many Christians (especially teenagers) seems more like a project, sale, or debate.

My son and his church friends were at a local fair and ran into a booth offering "salvation."

"This desire to remove anything extraneous from the system is called reductionism… in theory, companies can get more productivity out of laborers who waste no resources…in modern youth ministry, reductionism showed in our proclivity to purchase a program or curriculum, or take our kids to a really hyped-up rally rather than do the long, hard work of building relationships and sharing Christ over time."

—Tony Jones, theologian and author
Postmodern Youth Ministry

Despite a lengthy conversation, bordering on manipulation and argument that "our church" was full of false doctrine and this man's "church" was offering the "only way" to eternal life, the boys finally had enough. "He told me I wasn't saved," my son shared later. Fortunately, my boy is mature enough to know otherwise, but what about his friends? Too much of what passes as evangelism is sheep-stealing, sales quotas, and heated argument.

In contrast, an incarnational faith steps into the teenagers' world and walks alongside them. Remember Jesus' walking with his two followers on the road to Emmaus? They didn't know who this stranger was nor did they care. It's not like they invited Jesus to join them. These two followers were literally heartbroken. Despite rumors that Jesus was alive they still didn't believe it. Depressed, disillusioned, and now distancing themselves from the others, they walked away from Jerusalem. What did Jesus do? Did he argue or act condescendingly? Did he berate their lack of faith? Did he scold their selfishness? Did he stop them and point them back to Jerusalem? Did he give them a tract on 25 evidences Jesus is alive? Did he invite them to his rabbi's synagogue?

No. Jesus just walked with them. He joined them in their journey and simply listened. Sure, he comforted and encouraged them. He also gently reminded them of the Old Testament writings on the Messiah. He taught them like children—who were sad, scared, and struggling. Eventually Jesus revealed his true identity, and these two disciples returned to their faith.

If you want a picture of incarnational evangelism, this story is it. Jesus didn't wait for them. He didn't create a program for despondent disciples. He went after them, he walked with them, and he invested time and heart.

He waited until they were ready for him to reveal. Faith isn't some magic moment but a highway of markers and monuments. Evangelism starts not with your lips, but your life. It's showing up. It's touching base. It's looking a disappointed and discouraged student directly in the eye and saying nothing except "I know." We know what it's like to be a teenager. We know about prom night zits, unplanned pregnancies, peer pressure to drink, loneliness, insecurity, loss, and death.

Incarnational evangelism is well-suited for the smaller church because it's relational in context. Programs don't save. Arguments don't save. A tract won't save. What is most persuasive is a life that's changed by Jesus. It's his life on your life (and my life). It's relying on story not debate to share your faith.

Everybody has a faith story, but few youth groups encourage their kids or give them platforms to share their journey with God.

And if you can't confess your story with friends of faith, you'll rarely do it with friends without faith.

BECOMING MISSIONAL

The great "Go-Mission" in Matthew 28:18-20 is to go into the entire world and share the message of Jesus. It's not an option. It's not a gift given to just a few special believers. We're all commanded to evangelize, and we do that best by going somewhere. Anywhere.

Jesus modeled missional evangelism throughout his ministry. Yes, he taught in the synagogue every now and again, but most of his work happened in fields, on water, and beside hills. He went to people where they lived, worked, played, and ate.

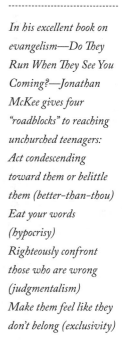

In his excellent book on evangelism—Do They Run When They See You Coming?—Jonathan McKee gives four "roadblocks" to reaching unchurched teenagers:
Act condescending toward them or belittle them (better-than-thou)
Eat your words (hypocrisy)
Righteously confront those who are wrong (judgmentalism)
Make them feel like they don't belong (exclusivity)

To be missional means we abandon the *Field of Dreams* approach to evangelism: *"If you build it they will come."* The church of the past 35 years has slowly adopted a dangerous consumer mindset that buildings and programs evangelize on their own power. We erect a bigger facility so we can save more people. Or we launch another program or ministry so we can win more souls. Youth ministries are constantly under the gun to draw more kids to the church building. Many pastors and church leaders won't even count attendance figures that happen away from the building. It's like the building is some sacred space and unless a student (or adult) starts, parks, or ends at the facility, it's not legitimate ministry.

Amen, brother Rick! Preach on!

The problem in 21C culture is the world no longer comes to the church. In fact, as we've already shared, there's significant evidence the church may have a negative reputation as spooky, seductive, or stodgy. Kid Rock confesses in his song "Amen" how he's afraid to send his kids to church because of "wolves in sheep clothes pastors." Television and films routinely paint a church building as a place you go for weddings and funerals and prayer but not much else.

Even church kids grow weary of faith being compartmentalized to a street address and time period.

A missional youth ministry operates wonderfully within a smaller church context because space and time are problems we'd love to leave behind and can if we're truly willing to participate in the "go-mission."

Laura is a volunteer youth leader for a small church of 75 in central Nebraska. She has only a scattered few teenagers that come to youth meetings on Sunday nights, and she's grown depressed and deeply discouraged. Why don't kids want to come back to church? When she was a teenager in the youth group Sunday nights were filled with games, food, and wonderful fellowship. Now nobody seems interested. The few that do come only do so because their parents have a leadership meeting at the church during the same time.

Then one day Laura was reading how Jesus rarely did ministry at the synagogue. He seemed to always be out in the community or in homes. Laura grew naturally frustrated that her meetings only happened at church, so she spoke to her leadership about trying something different: a Friday night gathering in her home. She'd feed the kids supper (if they wanted to join her) and then they'd play video games, watch television, or swim in her pool.

The evening would close with 30-45 minutes of Bible study and prayer. "You're still going to lead a Sunday night meeting right?" one leader asked. "No," replied Laura, "this weekly fellowship would replace Sunday night." She could see this didn't sit well with the leadership. They've always had a Sunday night meeting. However, after a lengthy discussion and debate, the church leaders relented and blessed her vision with prayer.

Laura's Friday night gatherings were attended initially by the same few regulars, but soon other kids caught wind of the Wii tourneys, pool parties, and supper and joined the group. The students felt right at home at Laura's place, and as she built deeper relationships she also felt more comfortable going deeper into their world. She ate lunch at their school and cheered at their games, and one Friday night they all headed to the mall for a movie.

So many of my friends are frustrated with their church experience. Many of them have left churches because the way they were treated in their youth group, not only be peers but also by adults."

—19-year-old
(Quoted by Mike King in *Presence-Centered Youth Ministry*)

Laura finally felt like she was doing youth ministry, and her few regulars had now grown to 15 strong. She even smiled when another church couple jumped in to help Laura cook and lead the group.

Six months later, the "gathering" started to meet in two different homes, then three, then four. Each group is strategically located in a neighborhood so church teenagers can invite friends who might never attend "church" to participate in an evening of games, food, and community. No group ever grows larger than 20 before forming another "gathering." The little church has also seen an attendance boost of around 50 people.

And it's all because Laura decided to think missionally. She adopted a Jesus strategy rather than sticking to business as usual. Laura thought outside the church box and discovered youth ministry happens in the streets, the homes, the mall, and the school.

The truly good news is that at least 10 teenagers have become followers of Jesus through these gatherings.

Laura has a lot in common with John Yokoyama, the owner of the Pike Place Fish Market. She discovered that evangelism isn't some program or product that can be shopped. Evangelism is a living attitude that roars within the soul of someone sensitive to his or her world. That's why in Acts 1:8 believers were commanded to share their faith story *first* in Jerusalem.

And why the Gadarene demoniac was told to go back to his family and tell the good news of his transformation (Mark 5:18-20). Evangelism begins in our backyard, in our cul-de-sac, in our neighborhood school, and in our community clubs. It starts with family and friends.

Just like the Pike Place Fish Market, smaller churches hold a decided advantage in the numbers game. Less is more. Evangelism is rooted in relationship, trust, story, and conversation. It's life on life, one person at a time. Listen again to John Yokoyama's quote about his fish market, except paraphrased through the eyes of the faith community:

> For us (the church) it means going beyond just providing outstanding service to people. It means really being present with people and relating to them as human beings (incarnational). You know, stepping outside the usual "we're in business and you're a customer" way of relating to people and intentionally being with them right now, in the present moment, person to person (incarnational). We take all our attention off ourselves to be only with them…looking for ways to serve them (missional). We're out to discover how we can make their day (missional).[10]

My brother Randy is a fish's worst nightmare. He's a hardcore outdoorsman who's so good at his craft others call him for counsel. Every August he connects with a "band of brothers" at Fort Stevens, Oregon, to battle the big ones. They live two weeks in campers and tents in order to catch the coho salmon, tuna, crab, and other fish currently running the Columbia River and the Pacific Ocean. They transport freezers to hold their meat, which are caught, filleted, and vacuum-packed to seal in their freshness.

It's quite an operation that nets dozens of fish every season.

The fish camp is always alive with stories. If you visit them, you'll hear tales about humpback whales, seals, and sharks. You'll dine on fresh crab and salmon for supper.

[10]http://www.pikeplacefish.com/About-Us-3.html

You'll hear yarns about past trophy catches and hear lectures on tidal flows, barometric pressure, blessed herring, and countless other tips to guarantee success. After supper the men gather around a laptop to view dozens of digital fishing photos—and tell more stories. My brother has confessed he'd fish year-round if he could. It's his passion.

I find the enthusiasm these men hold for the hunt somewhat amusing. Frankly, I like to fish but I'm not a fanatic about it. Fishing is messy and smelly, and you have to sacrifice a lot of time and good money. I don't mind watching an occasional fishing show, but I'm not going to spend hours doing research at the Outdoor Channel (like my brother). Plus, to catch the coho you have to wake at 'o dark thirty and boat up to two hours just to *start* fishing. I'll even confess to a somewhat sour attitude about fishing. I can think of dozens of other things I'd rather do. I'm not very good, hate getting wet, and hold little affection for making God's little creatures bleed for my supper.

Consequently, I don't catch a lot of fish. Now, if they'd just jump in my boat I'd probably head to the lake, river, or ocean more often, but successful fishing requires patience, perseverance, and perspective.

It's no secret that you catch fish in bodies of water. You have to go to their culture, seek them, bait them, hook them, and reel them in. You have to *think* like a fish. What do they like? What gets their attention? You don't catch fish parked at your kitchen table. And fishing is always better with friends.

But as one of my brother's buddies shared, "too many lines make a miserable mess."

Too many poles on a boat mean snags, crossed lines, and other trouble.

Too many boats fishing the same water creates congestion and confusion.

Fishing is best done *small* with a few faithful friends on mission.

Similarly, evangelism is soaked in relational experience. It's sharing your story—good and bad—in conversation and community. A 21C culture leery of religious lures and hooks won't bite much on our message. The era of mass evangelism is over. Christian conversion that lasts is rooted in friendship. It's why small is tall. Like a fish camp operates best with only a few, so does sharing your faith succeed through the context of a smaller church youth ministry.

Jesus called us to fish for people.

Unfortunately, for many church kids (and adult leaders) evangelism is "messy and smelly and a waste of time." But I suspect the reason we don't truly share our faith is we don't know how, our attitude is sour, and our evangelism experiences have been miserable. We've dropped our lines and nobody bit.

We've baited our hooks with PowerPoints, flashy stories, and clever apologetics only to find teenagers, friends, and family members repelled by our tactics. The fish finder shows plenty of possibility, but we're dragging tinfoil entertainment and toothpick truth wondering why nobody gets it.

One of my favorite fish stories is John 21, just after Jesus has appeared to his followers alive. Peter decides to clear his mind the only way he knows: fishing. Nathaniel, Thomas, James, John, and two other disciples think that's a splendid idea and they head to the open waters to drop nets, talk shop, smell the air, cool down, and get perspective.

They fished all night long and caught zip, but like most fishermen they know this happens from time to time.

Sometimes you score and limit out. Sometimes you head home empty-handed. Then, in the morning twilight, a stranger shows up and instructs them to cast their nets on the other side of the boat. Of course, to any experienced fisherman this is an example of insanity: casting the same place with expectation of different result. What's this shore-hugger know that we don't? It's a lot of work to recast the nets, and it's not like we're going to new fishing waters.

But what did they have to lose? Faith emerges out of failure.

So they move their nets a few feet to the other side of the boat and within minutes are slamming fish in such numbers they can't even haul in their catch. Peter immediately recognizes the stranger is Jesus and jumps overboard, swimming to shore. You see, he's been carrying some heavy emotional baggage for days now, the type that drags you to the bottom of life. He did what he swore he'd never do: deny his friend—and not just once but three times in a single night.

Peter is depressed, discouraged, and disappointed but smart enough to still know he needs a savior.

When Peter reaches shore Jesus is enjoying a fish sandwich for breakfast, cooking it on a fire of "burning coals." The Greek here is very insightful as the word for "burning coals" appears only one other place in John's Gospel: back before the crucifixion of Jesus when Peter is warming himself around a fire ("burning coals") in John 18:18. This is the setting for Peter's first denial. Around the flicker of firelight, Peter will lie about knowing Jesus. He'll disown his master.

Peter will play politics to save his own skin.

Jesus begins the restoration process by bringing Peter back to the scene of his crime, and then asks him three times, *"Do you love me?"* Jesus tags on a commission for this fisherman to become a shepherd. He doesn't denounce, criticize, complain, berate, or guilt Peter. He just looks at him eyeball to eyeball over a bed of burning coals and says, "I know." For every time Peter denied Jesus he's asked about his love. Peter doesn't get it at first (most of us don't) but eventually Jesus pats Peter on the back with a new purpose to go.

It's the Christian life in a nutshell: Love Jesus and feed people spiritual food. Jesus had to "re-evangelize" Peter that day, not unlike what you'll have to do with your churched teenagers. Jesus restored Peter in grace and gave him a "go-mission." Jesus didn't wait for Peter to seek him out. He didn't lecture him with spiritual laws, debate him with fish apologetics, or hand him a tract on "fishing for life." Jesus met Peter in the fire of doubt and disappointment to set him ablaze with possibility and purpose.

That's how you fish for people. It's why *small is tall*. You can't manufacture these types of miraculous moments through a crowd. It's life on life. It's looking into the eyes of a teenager and saying, "I know." It's sharing a meal, telling a story, creating a memory, and opening a heart to a new mission. It's heading to the lake, getting your hands smelly, and finding purpose in your nets.

You have a lot of advantages and opportunities to change lives for Jesus in the smaller church context. Do you love the master fisherman? Do you really love the Messiah? Do you truly *love* the king?

Then *feed* his teenagers—and become "world famous!"

Steph's 2Cents

I am SO pumped now! Loving the whole "Friday nights at Laura's house" story. So, let's do it. Let's create our own Friday night dinner event together. It'll keep us accountable to getting it done PLUS we can share our stories with each other on the smallchurchyouthministry.com blog. For right now, I'm thinking we start with the first one and we'll see how it goes from there.

Every successful event begins with a planning list; feel free to use this as a template for all your youth events.

Date

We're excited about this now so six weeks out is too far away! But two weeks is not enough notice to maximize getting all our kids there. I'm thinking three or four weeks from now sounds good. Gives us a fair shot at utilizing all the "in-house" church publications plus any other creative ways of getting the word out. I'm also going to double-check that the Friday night I pick isn't homecoming, prom, or something big like that.

Time

Carve out a 2- to 2.5-hour time slot. Based on Laura's story, I'm thinking we should figure in 45 minutes for dinner. After all, I want to sit long enough to hear my kids' stories. Try to get everyone around one table. I'm putting out table discussion tent cards with two or three really fun or quirky questions to get the conversation started. Better yet, I'll probably connect the questions to something I'll use in the lesson time later.

What if we budget an hour for the fun time? Maybe some TV, card/board game, half a movie, Guitar Hero, decorate my Christmas tree, whatever.

Laura's use of a 30-45 minute lesson is a good estimate. We have to make sure we as leaders aren't talking the whole time. Our job is to facilitate so we get our students talking. Swapping fish stories, so to speak!

Location

I have a great setup for this in my home. The kitchen is right off the dining/living/family areas. It's all connected and I've had teenagers over before where several smaller groups broke out—but they were still together. Only you can decide if you can make your place work. The number one goal is for a unity of group in a unity of space. If your place won't work, find someone else's home where the homeowner AND the kids will feel comfortable.

Who to Invite

Adults: Which other significant adults you invite depends on your programming setup.

The basic rules would be:

1. You can't be the only adult.

2. There has to be an adult of the opposite sex if you have youth of the opposite sex.

3. There should be another adult who doesn't already live there or is related to you.

4. Any other key church adults involved in the lives of your kids would really benefit from this experience—like their Sunday school teacher or the youth choir director. Be careful, though, not to make this SO adult heavy that the students feel overwhelmed. It won't set an "open-up" environment.

Youth: Here is where the joy of working with a smaller number of kids is a REAL blessing. Invite every teenager you can think of who is connected to your church. Don't limit it to just those regulars at your weekly group meeting.

"On the rolls" church no-shows might just show up to something like this out of pure curiosity or because their folks made them! Should kids bring a friend? I'd say yes, but this is a decision up to you based on your purpose and place. You might decide that friends are best invited at the second dinner. This gives you a chance to use the first dinner as a "figure it out" practice run.

Communication

Studies show that people need to hear about an event five times before they really "hear" about the event. My suggestions for this event?

1. Send personal "in the mail" invitations

2. E-mail parents so they know what's up and help their kids make it happen

3. Use the church bulletin/newsletter/website so everyone else knows what's going on with the youth

4. Post info on your youth group Facebook page and website

5. E-mail or text RSVP reminders to youth

What to Eat

Not fish! (Though I'm hungry for salmon after reading this chapter.) You want kids to enjoy the dinner and you want them to come back again. The kids will LOVE you (no matter what they say) if you can claim bragging rights for preparing the meal. This first time is not an "order pizza" night, either. Some form of Italian is a safe bet served with salad, garlic bread, and dessert. I HATE to cook so I'm buying the big trays of lasagna from "you-know-where" that just heat up in the oven. If I asked, I have parents who would bring the other stuff. To show my love, I'm setting the table, too, candles and all.

What to Talk About

I want to talk about what the kids are talking about. What's the latest buzz topic? What's all over the news right now? Pick a really timely topic and craft three to five GREAT questions. What makes for a productive question? Ones that can't be answered with yes or no so nothing that begins with can, should, would, or does. Really great questions are surprising, personal, and specific. An average question sounds like this: What makes for a good best friend? A question that follows the three guidelines above sounds like this: When does your best friend make you the happiest, and why?

Clean up/Evaluate

Ask your adults ahead of time to stay an extra half-hour to evaluate the night. Washing and drying dishes is great conversation time. Talk about what worked; what could be tweaked if you do this again? Gives the adults "buy-in" from that moment on.

Follow up

Emily Post would say the kids should send you a thank you but you and I know that ain't gonna happen. A surprising twist for your kids is for you to send them a thank you instead—sooner than later, so I'd say an online greeting card will suffice. My kids still love getting those from me.

CHAPTER SEVEN ◎ FIRE STARTERS!

> But if I say I'll never mention the Lord or speak in his name, his word burns in my heart like a fire. It's like a fire in my bones! I am worn out trying to hold it in! I can't do it! (Jeremiah 20:9 NLT).
>
> But a tiny spark can set a great forest on fire (James 3:5b NLT).
>
> "A glimpse of God will save you. To gaze at him will sanctify you."
> —Manley Beasley

Few things are more awe-inspiring and awful than a forest fire. In a matter of minutes a runaway blaze can torch everything in its path, leaving nothing but stone and ashes. A fire breathes on its own and has personality. It flames, flickers, and flashes. It doesn't discriminate and will incinerate a gorgeous California suburb as easily as it consumes wilderness backcountry. Monster fires kill but also create long overdue change. A fire that turns a forest into ashes might be the catalyst for new growth.

A fire is certainly destructive, but biologists readily admit it's a necessary evil for wildlife and forest management. We fight fires differently today than we did 40 years ago. For much of the 20th century, it was national policy to suppress a forest fire by 10 a.m. the next day. Smoke jumpers parachuted into remote areas to quench blazes before they erupted into major and unstoppable forces. This policy emerged in response to two of our nation's worst fires: the 1871 Wisconsin's Peshtigo fire (which killed 1,500 people) and the Great Fire of 1910 (an out-of-control Montana/Idaho fire that destroyed more than 3 million acres and killed 86). Conventional wisdom and policy argued that it was important to keep fires small and controlled.

The problem is, fire also cleanses a forest of dead stuff. When a fire is suppressed it can't do what nature intended.

Consequently, starting in the early 1970s, a certain number of "prescribed natural fires" were eventually allowed to burn under a watchful eye and during moist conditions. These fires eliminated old growth trees, dry tinder, and other forest fuels that burn hot and rapid.

But this doesn't guarantee disasters won't happen. In 1988, Yellowstone National Park was decimated by one of the worst forest fires in history. It started as several small fires due mostly to dry lightning strikes that ignited forests decimated by extended drought and beetle-infested dead trees. When high winds fanned these smaller fires into one huge firestorm it burned for months and charred nearly 800,000 acres or over one-third of the park. In fact, there were almost 250 fires in Yellowstone and surrounding forests in 1988, including the seven that eventually morphed into the monster park fire.

The problem in 1988 was the severe western drought that baked Yellowstone forests into conditions ripe for disaster. Therefore, when dry lightning sparked flames and winds whipped up embers high into the air to other locations, the Great Yellowstone Fire of 1988 exploded and burned uncontrollably for weeks. In fact, Mother Nature herself cooled the fires with late September rains and lower temps. As catastrophic as the Yellowstone fire proved to be, there were more than 72,000 wildfires reported that same year, including 300 major fires nationally.

The 1988 Yellowstone fires are a living testimony to how small sparks can eventually create massive revival. Yes, I did say *revival*.

After all, if you visit Yellowstone today, you'll witness a park that enjoys a much healthier ecosystem. Sure, there are remnants of blackened lodge pole pine trees still standing like toothpick memorials to the fire, but few would argue the benefits of the blaze. Even reports of wildlife killed in the fires were minimal, and not one of Yellowstone's precious grizzly population died in the inferno. In fact, within days after the fire passed through a region, grizzlies were grazing the barbequed leftovers. Today, the wildlife is healthier and abundant in the regions scarred most by the fires.

What seemed to be tragic has become triumph.

EMERGING WORSHIP

In many ways a worship firestorm is torching church as we know it and threatens "old growth" preferences, styles, and strategies. Conventional wisdom argues to quench these new "fires" of expression and even to tag them as evil, New Age, or touchy-feely, but the culture of emerging generations suggests a change is coming. Smaller churches are naturally sized to embrace newer worship strategies and create attractive environments that lead people into a deeper personal experience with God.

As part of a modern architecture, worship has been built upon a passive, word-oriented mechanism that remains popular even in some of our largest churches. I like to call it "Woodstock Worship"—named after the boomer generation's affection for bands, background singers, and righteous rock 'n' roll. "Woodstock Worship" is the heart and soul of the boomer church, particularly the graying megachurch, and found its roots in the early '70s Jesus movement.

"Tradition is the living faith of the dead, traditionalism is the dead faith of the living."

—Jaroslav Pelikan, university professor and author

Christian "hippie" converts, particularly in Southern California, literally launched a new type of "Jesus music" and rewrote the church hymnal ("Just As I Am" morphed into "Seek Ye First"). This worship revolution found its tipping point in the mid-1980s as boomers ascended into church leadership and influenced traditional worship styles. Many congregations endured bitter battles (a.k.a. "worship wars") as hymns, hymnals, and the church organist were replaced by praise choruses, hand-raising, PowerPoint slides, and full bands.

Throughout the 1980s, the genre of "contemporary Christian music" continued to feed the church with new praise anthems like Rich Mullin's "Awesome God" and Michael W. Smith's "Great is the Lord." By the mid-1990s, worship became a contemporary Christian music buzzword, largely driven by an emerging generation of Gen X believers who hungered for something deeper than a praise chorus mantra. In youth ministry conferences and leadership conventions a fresh worship spirit was blowing, featuring music by new artists like David Crowder, Matt Redman, and Chris Tomlin. Even established artists like the Newsboys joined newer groups in releasing worship albums.

In local youth ministries, especially in larger churches, student bands blossomed to play these new tunes and innovate a fresh energy of worship that attracted adolescents to church. It also created a space for the musically talented teenagers to share their skill, since many school systems were dropping music programs due to budget cuts. The church was filling a neighborhood cultural need.

If you truly want to see the evolution of worship among younger generations, simply review the concert history of U2 (the Gen X "Beatles").

In fact, the predominant hymn of the emerging generations might be the band's 1987 hit song "I Still Haven't Found What I'm Looking For." U2's spiritual element (three members of the band profess Christianity) combined with its innate ability to surf cultural edges and move popular music in new directions is unparalleled.

Years	Albums	Live Concert	Worship Lyric/ Theme	Impact on Adolescent Worship
1980-1983	*Boy, October, War*	Red Rocks concert sparks several "worship" moments when U2 performs in a cold rain to thousands of loyal fans	*"I will sing a new song, how long to sing this song? ("40")*	Teenagers want more out of worship than singing a song in a pew. They want a cause to believe in.
1984-1989	*Unforgettable Fire, Joshua Tree, Rattle and Hum*	During Live Aid concert in 1985, Bono jumps off stage to dance with fan and starts a U2 tradition.	*"In the name of love, what more in the name of love" "(Pride) In The Name of Love"*	Teenagers hunger to worship through a relationship, to touch God and feel his presence.
1990-1993	*Achtung Baby, Zooropia*	The 1992-1993 Zoo TV Tour created a multimedia visual event with live satellite	*"Love is a temple, Love a higher law,... You ask me to enter but then you make me crawl" ("One")*	Teenagers are aided in worship by the use of multi-visuals.
1994-1999	*Pop*	Popmart tour (1997) is Zoo TV, part two. Many question U2's ability to stay culturally hip.	*"You're looking for the one but you know you're somewhere else instead. You want to be the song, be the song that you hear in your head." ("Discotheque")*	The great worship marketing years. Youth leaders create worship events and purchase worship resources. The rise of new worship music.

2000-2006	All You Can't Leave Behind, How To Dismantle an Atomic Bomb	U2 returns to smaller arenas "leaving behind" the arenas and releases a 3-D concert movie (the first of a new, but old, genre).	"Hello, Hello Hola! I'm at a place called vertigo (¿Dónde está?) [Where is it?]! It's everything I wish I didn't know, except you give me something I can feel" ("Vertigo")	Worship begins to emerge as an experiential, participatory event that includes candles, incense, prayer stations/labyrinths, and interactive moments.
2007 – Present	No Line On The Horizon	U2 embarks on 360° Tour (2009) in which the audience is seated completely around the band and the largest concert stage every constructed. U2 is a must-see live act despite falling album sales.	"I was born to sing for you, I didn't have a choice but to lift you up and sing whatever song you wanted me to. I give you back my voice from the womb. My first cry, it was a joyful noise" ("Magnificent")	Worship is a participatory, experiential and image-soaked event that's both large and small at the same time. Worship exists for God not humanity.

Many smaller churches have found themselves far behind the curve in worship, due to facility limitations, a lack of worship specialists/musical talent, financial resources to purchase projection/audio equipment, or simply staunch church tradition. In many smaller congregations the worship still trends to mid-80s "contemporary" and features a blend of hymns and praise choruses. Sometimes the cultural setting holds a smaller church worship back. My family lived for four years in eastern Appalachian, small-town Kentucky. Unlike the larger city churches a mere 45 minutes away, most of these congregations still used organists, hymns, and church choirs for worship experiences. It was contextualized to the culture. Eastern Kentucky lived 20 years behind the rest of the world, and church worship reflected it.

The value of a dynamic smaller church youth ministry is its opportunity to feed the entire congregation new songs to sing. Worship isn't static and like a fire will explode and go where it wants. In a smaller context, worship can adopt more relational strategies and unleash deeper experiential moments. It's not about a show or a band or a PowerPoint. Authentic worship is messy and mistake-ridden. It's David dancing in his underwear. It's a prostitute wiping Jesus' feet with tears. It's Zacchaeus finding Jesus in a tree. Authentic worship focuses less on entertainment excellence and more upon moments of spiritual connection. It's not about hitting all the notes but nailing the relational component that melds a person's heart to the Father's throne.

One of the misguided notions in smaller churches is worship should be "perfect" and "programmed." But like a fire in a forest, you can't predict the Spirit's blaze. He may dance in one heart and harden another. He might free one person but fetter another. The Holy Spirit can't be expunged and will thrive wherever there's fuel and freedom. When we try to capture worship and contain it within a liturgy or program, we quench the Spirit's potential and rob God of his majesty. We douse the Spirit's power to move where we don't want him to move. We smother the Spirit's promise to renew, refresh, restore, reinvigorate, and reform.

So your youth ministry's worship is a bit ugly? *Good.* So the band lacks real talent? *Great.* Sing a new song anyway. So what if it's too loud or fails to impress the critics. All you need is authentic, gutsy, flawed worship with hearts open and willing to let the Spirit lead. Of course there are some advantages to being small in worship expression. Smaller church youth ministries can easily ignite powerful worship moments simply by focusing upon a relational, experiential, and image-soaked strategy.

RELATIONAL WORSHIP

Most adult worship services are non-relational and non-participatory. It's "sit-and-soak" worship. One of my favorite pastimes is to visit churches and watch the people worship. In some churches, everyone sings a "joyful sound" but in other places few people participate or sing. In fact, in some worship settings it's now a "tradition" to stand while the song service is in session. If you don't stand, the worship leader usually gives a gentle nudge to stand. Why? Is it because standing is more spiritual? Or because it gives the "illusion" that people are actually participating?

The goal of relational worship is to connect teenagers to each other for deeper communion and conversation. It's not a passive "sit-and-soak" worship event but one rich in participation. Relational and participatory worship eliminates walls and builds bridges. And it's no surprise it's highly effective within smaller numbers.

EXPERIENTIAL WORSHIP

Personal experience is how emerging generations gravitate toward truth. Therefore, the best apologetic for a living relationship with God is a powerful moment when a person uniquely senses God's presence. You might say we *feel* our way toward God more than we *think* our way to him. That thought might be unnerving, but most of our ideas about God (a.k.a. theology) are rooted in experiences. Our frame for God as "Father" emerges from our relationship with our earthly dad. Our view of the church sprouts from our experiences *in* church. Every attitude, value, or feeling—good or bad—creates the voice we trust.

This is the value of experiential worship and strategies that touch the senses, both individually and corporately.

Experiential worship is also participatory in nature and focuses upon creating authentic connections to God. Worship can be experiential using objects to invoke insight and idea. You can also enjoy experiential worship in unique places. I've taken my youth groups to graveyards, gas stations, zoos, ponds, garbage dumps, malls, fast food restaurants, city parks, and roller rinks to "experience" worship and teach biblical truth.

You've heard the world is the classroom? It's also a chapel.

IMAGE-SOAKED WORSHIP

Do you remember the last time you bought a new car—or a new-to-you car? As you took your first drives, you probably started to notice that a lot of other people were driving the same car, even though you hadn't noticed it a week or month earlier. Obviously, they all didn't go out and buy cars the same day you did—what happened was your perspective had changed. Your eyes adapted a new frame of reference and you saw things you hadn't seen before.

Worship touches all the senses, but the eyes are particularly receptive. It's one of the reasons experiential worship works so well. When we worship visually we can see God work. Images unleash imagination. When we worship and sing about "mountains and oceans" the images help us get high and wet. When we meditate on Christ's forgiveness, an image of Jesus on a cross helps us live the moment. That's the power of image— especially moving images. We begin to "see" things about God that we hadn't seen before.

How can smaller youth ministries create an image-soaked worship environment? Moving images are the norm. Our eyes actually bore quickly with static images, unless it invokes an emotion. Consequently, images projected for worship need to be thoughtfully emotional. Just projecting words on a blank blue PowerPoint background won't cut it. A static photograph needs to change with every line in a song to hold attention and keep the imagination active. Or better yet, use a moving image as a backdrop so when you sing about "mountains and oceans" the students are transported via film clips of peaks and waves. Many creative types have remixed clips from *The Passion of the Christ* for use as meditations. YouTube is a tremendous resource for free worship clips, including beautiful movies to popular worship songs. You don't need a band, just a good way to project the clip.

A portable video projector is an excellent investment for any smaller church (current models are now under $500), not just for worship but educational and entertainment use. Since many teenagers own laptops for school and can create PowerPoint files and elements, there's no need for you to build the worship slides either. Use Google image searches to find powerful photos. Download and insert YouTube videos easily by using a free converter site like www.keepit.com. You can also purchase numerous photo and video backgrounds specially designed for worship. And since many smaller churches already use software that can include worship slides, you might already have access to this resource.

Not all small churches are lucky enough to have a projector. Mine does, but it's mounted on the ceiling and we don't have another one available for portable use. Don't feel bad—lots of small church youth groups don't have a projector. Don't be afraid to use a TV/laptop setup and if that's also non-existent, then there's always sock puppets. Just kidding!

Not really. I actually used sock puppets in worship one time quite successfully.

Of course, you don't need technology to soak your worship with images. In fact, many of the best worship experiences are completely unplugged. The church for centuries used visual images—especially stained glass, candles, and icons—to help worshipers understand theological truth and connect them to God (and you can too). Use candles to symbolize the presence of the Holy Spirit. Distribute objects like candy, spices, nails, tools, or crosses to serve as visual worship aids.

Many smaller churches enjoy midweek communion experiences and use the bread and fruit of the vine to instruct about the body and blood of Christ. A Jewish Passover is completely image-soaked. Every part of the ritual uses an object—from bitter herbs to roasted lamb to clothing—to teach the Exodus. What objects from your present could you use to remind teenagers of the past?

One of the reasons emerging generations have left the church in droves is they no longer feel God's presence in our worship and programs. We can argue, criticize, and dismiss that idea but there's truth to be learned in their departure. Younger generations hunger for a faith that burns authentic. They want to touch the flame. They want to be engulfed in something greater than their own existence. They want to be consumed by God's grace and charred by his justice.

It's why smaller congregations possess so much possibility and why youth ministry is the spark of change. No, we may not have all the cool resources, the musical talent, or the amazing worship facilities but we have something better: the opportunity to lead teenagers into a messy, murky, and marvelous connection with their heavenly Father.

"Worship services that are not worshipful, people not meeting God, people not being allowed to participate in a worship relationship with God—it is as if the very essence of worship has been quietly removed. Whenever we deplete worship there is a consequence, and we are now experiencing it. People are awakening from the entertainment-induced trance…and asking 'Is that all there is?'"

—Sally Morgenthaler, worship consultant and author *Worship Evangelism*

Relationships aren't perfect. In fact, authentic worship that attracts and engages will be remarkably unbalanced and off kilter. Ultimately worship happens in your heart, not your head. That's why you can't program worship. You can't plan God's presence. All you can do is create a worshipful environment and pray he shows up.

And of course he will..."where two or three are gathered."

The most common Greek word for worship is *proskuneo* or "to lean forward and kiss." Worship is a smooch on God's cheek. It's a slobbery smack that often misses the mark. Sometimes we just give a peck on the forehead. Sometimes we get lost in our lip-service. And occasionally we enjoy an intimate moment with our Creator. It's the kind of experience that brings tears, laughter, peace, and friendship. Worship is an emotional relationship.

Fantastic kisses tend to spread like wildfire. In Scripture "fire" is routinely connected to God's presence and personal worship. Moses and the burning bush. Shadrach, Meshach, and Abednego in a fiery furnace. Elijah and a chariot of fire. Apostles with tongues of fire on Pentecost.

Fire purifies. Fire destroys. Fire prepares.

Authentic worship is no different. And the good news? It only takes a spark.

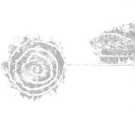

Steph's 2Cents

Funny you should end with that quote, Rick. There was this song that was ALL the rage in youth groups during the '70s and early '80s called "Pass It On." I remember it well. Picture it: I'm sitting in circle of my youth group friends around the campfire at the end of a retreat. Our arms are around one another's shoulders, and a tear trickles down my face. Not sure if the tear was from the power of the moment or the impending goodbyes to a boy I had met that weekend. The end result was the same: It's a few decades later and I still remember the scenario. (And the boy's name? It was Jeff—I think.) My point? The memory has lasted all these years because something connected in my heart and soul that day.

Part of my role on my church staff is serving on the creative planning team as the director of contemporary worship. Here are seven blanks we try to fill in when we want to light a fire under our worship planning. Save the headings and use them as a tool to help you spark your worship planning:

Theme

Ask yourself, "What's the one thing I want my kids to walk away with today?" Sum it up in one sentence, and then narrow it down even more. "God loves us" or "Jesus is the Resurrection" are WAY too broad. "You're blessed when you're at the end of your rope" (The first beatitude from Matthew 5:3, from The Message) is a doable concept for an hour's worth of time.

Imagery

To help your kids make the connection to the takeaway from your worship time, pick an easy-to-develop visual for your theme—something that's easy to find and can be used on a worship table, in slides, and is an actual touchable item.

149

Let's keep developing the beatitude idea. You could use a frayed rope or a big rock. I'm thinking about making this a four-week series on "How Your Attitude Should Be," so I'm going with the rock idea. On the worship table, I'll start with something as a foundation that says, "Blessed are" and then write each beatitude on a different large stone. Eventually, the stones will stack up like a mountain making the "Sermon on the Mount" tie-in.

Visuals

Even though the learning retention from dramas and video clips is only 40-50 percent, it's still enough to warrant weaving them into your youth services. Tell the message in five different ways within the worship time for the point to get across to everyone. I like to use clips, and for this service we're creating, I found a great clip on sermonspice.com called "Poor in Spirit," a perfect fit for the beatitude point.

Music

Unless your small group has been gifted with a young Chris Tomlin or Matt Redman, having live music in your group can be tough. If your worship time is new, you may not want to introduce group singing immediately. Wait until the time's right; otherwise it can be awkward and set you back. (I learned this the HARD way.) Using well-chosen music tracks to match the theme will work nicely in the early stages. You'll find great worship music clips at sermonspice.com and other worship media sites. As your kids become comfortable with the songs and a few favorites rise to the top, you can quietly start to sing along. They'll join you. What songs would I pick? For this service I'm thinking either Bebo Norman's "I Will Lift My Eyes," "The Valley Song" by Jars of Clay, or maybe "Mighty to Save" by Hillsong. A year from now, who knows?

Environment

You and I know God can be worshiped anywhere, but when you have a small crew, your own church can be the most difficult place to create a meaningful worship setting. Our church has a sanctuary built for 400 people so an appropriately sized space is a challenge to our youth group size.

Find a space in your church you can work with. Bring the space in through the use of things like a special rug, chair placement, pillows, candle screens, display boards with pictures, and so on. Provide a worship table or focal point, and make sure to weave your theme's visual into the setting.

Experiential

Want to give your students experiential worship? Get them inside the point of the Scripture. Help them feel, taste, see, sense, smell Jesus' story. Videos and visuals won't do it alone; be intentional about building in an experience where students make their own personal discoveries within the story and then worship the writer.

Back to the "Poor in Spirit" theme. I'm creating ideas around rocks, so time to open up my brain and grab creative ideas. I look inward, pray for vision, and then open up to a free-floating creative place. What comes to mind?

OK, what about using a big rock or something really heavy for kids to pick up, hold, and move? Kids will need someone else to help them carry the load. (See where this is going already?)

Application Questions

(Yes you can talk to each other during worship.) What rocky situations in your life feel like they're too big for God to pick up, and why? When your life is in a really rocky place (poor in spirit) what would you like God to do? What kind of prayer might you pray if you're in the middle of a rocky situation?

What "heavenly" results could come from your situation?

With quiet music playing, the teenagers each get a small rock and time to pray about their "poor in spirit" points. After a few minutes, I'll ask them to picture Jesus holding their rock instead. Then I'll invite them to connect with Jesus and when they're ready, to leave their rocks on the worship table as a way of leaving it to Jesus, the rock.

OK, that's off the top of my head. You can fine tune it for your setting.

CHAPTER EIGHT ◎ FACEBOOK ROCKS!

In the world of physics, everything has changed.

As we've improved scientific process, we've discovered life is not either/or but both/and. We exist within a chaotic multi-verse (not uni-verse)—simple and complex, liquid and solid, moving and static. Quantum physics has replaced Newtonian ideas about how the smallest pieces of subatomic matter interact and relate.

In Newton's "closed" universe the world was foundational and featured "building blocks" of mechanism and control. Structural silos demarcated knowledge into various disciplines: the study of life (biology), the study of the soul (psychology), the study of God (theology), the study of humanity (sociology). These closed systems not only defined and framed life in order to understand it, but also created the illusion that we could intentionally manipulate (program) the silo to produce results. Darwinian evolution operates well within a closed universe, as does Skinnerian behaviorism. If we're nothing but highly evolved animals, it's OK to treat people like dogs (here's a treat for being good, Fido).

[1]Margaret J. Wheatley, *Leadership and the New Science: Discovering Order in a Chaotic World* (San Francisco: Berrett-Koehler Publishers, 1999): 20.

These Newtonian ideas impacted philosophy, business, education, entertainment, media, and even the church for hundreds of years.

The Industrial Revolution emerged as a glorious machine that produced *results.* Suddenly the bottom line was all that mattered. The assembly line strategy wasn't just good business but proved effective in education, as we moved from one-room schoolhouses to age-grade learning. In the 20th century church, we also adopted structural mechanisms, results-oriented, principled, and purpose-driven strategies. We boxed our worship into time and space (10:30 a.m. Sundays) forcing a "go to church" mentality. We purchased curriculum "scope and sequence" to program spiritual growth. We built staff and innovated ministry silos: children's ministry, youth ministry, adult ministry, singles ministry, senior saint ministry, worship team ministry, building and grounds ministry, ad nauseam. The modern church still reflects this Newtonian design. There's an order of service. Membership rolls and rules. Senior pastor. Programmed strategies. Denominations. Job descriptions. Church growth principles.

IT'S A NEW WORLD

However, in Einstein's world of relativity and quantum physics, we're discovering relationship matters more than results. In fact, you can have a great product without anyone knowing you exist—and conversely a poor product that everybody blogs to avoid! Quantum physics proposes an open "multi-verse" where everything is connected. When a butterfly flaps its wings in Argentina a hurricane can happen in the Atlantic.

It doesn't mean that there's no longer structure or order, but that we understand "order" through "dis-order" (a.k.a. chaos theory). We define "structure" by the relationships and experiences that create them (often more through failure, crisis, bloodshed, tears, and pain than success, safety, progress, and health).

In philosophical circles this has introduced the idea of "deconstructionism," which is nothing more than "standing under" something in order to understand it. If we want to comprehend, we need to rip away the prejudices, biases, and experiences that frame the lens. Is the sky "blue?" Well, yes and no. It's "blue" because in our cultural context (education, experience, family) we've been told that color is "blue." But what if "blue" was "orange" in a different culture and the frame to define that color was also atypical? Just because we say it's "blue" doesn't make it "blue." We must deconstruct how we came to understand this color to be "blue" in the first place. To understand, we must stand under and remove the frames that create the truth. Sounds messy, doesn't it? Exactly.

This is the heart of the controversy with "objective" truth or reality. It's just another silo. It's just another frame that someone says is "objective" (whatever that *means*). Objective truth is an illusion carved by our community and context and yet, in reality, it's subjective to our personal experience.

In the emerging world—the social culture our teenagers are inheriting—this paradox is appreciated and even valued. But don't misunderstand a deeper insight: Just because objectivity is rejected doesn't mean Absolute Truth has necessarily been abandoned, too. *The X-Files* noted "the truth is out there," and this is both the bane and beauty of ministry to emerging generations.

"…postmoderns are no longer convinced that their world has a center or that human reason can perceive any logical structure in the external universe. They live in a world in which the distinction between truth and fiction has evaporated. Consequently, they become collectors of experiences, repositories of transitory, fleeting images produced and fostered by the diversity of media forms endemic in postmodern society."

—Stanley Grenz, theologian and author
A Primer on Postmodernism

I've heard many misguided rants that today's kids reject objective truth as if they're also snubbing Absolute Truth, but that's an erroneous perception. Few teenagers will argue they "know" that "there is no God" as this is an absolute statement and requires omniscience to confirm! In reality, emerging generations reflect an Einstein open-source, multi-verse world.

They build their truth (perceptions, values, ideas) based upon experience and community. It's "my" truth because all I know is "my" truth. Like Paul shared with the Corinthians, what we know now "is partial and incomplete," but we will someday experience Absolute Truth "with perfect clarity."

Which is why you can't *program* spirituality. When we silo faith into clever clichés, pet doctrines, denominational curriculum, preaching topics, and a calendar of spiritual activity, we reduce faith to a frame that limits connection and community. Suddenly the lesson manual is more important than the individual and the event is more significant than the student. If you grew up in the church you know this is true. What truly remain are the people, not the programs. We recall the experience, the context, the feelings, and the changes these events, activities, and lessons caused. We remember the *mess* and the *message* and the *Messiah*.

If we've learned anything from the failing of youth ministry in the past 20 years it's the myth that programs are the end all, be all. It's a bit like the chicken and the egg. Do we program to *reach* students? Or do our programs merely *reflect* a community need? Let me put it a different way. Do we *start a program with a few* to attract more? Or do we develop a *strategy from within our community* that draws a few? Need me to be more specific? OK. Where do your program ideas emerge?

Do your ideas come from a box, a conference, a youth expert, a book, or a website, or do you develop experiences based upon conversation, conflict, and community with students in your neighborhood?

Now do you see the difference?

Smaller church youth ministries will be very effective in 21C culture when they finally eliminate the need to import their programs.

A program isn't bad, except out of context—and many are just that! And as mentioned, you can't program or force-feed spirituality. At best, you can create attractive, engaging environments where spiritual things happen (and usually in a surprising way), but you can't kick-start a youth program like some old motorcycle. That's Newtonian youth ministry, and it'll fail every time.

FACEBOOK YOUTH MINISTRY

What we need is the smaller church to lead through a different dimension. We don't need a new frame, lens, program, or system. We don't need to think outside the box. We need to operate as if there are no boxes. That's open-source, multi-verse, paradoxical, and fluid youth ministry.

The purpose for spiritual activity (events, experiences, lessons, messages) in 21C culture is to develop relationships and deepen community. In fact, the only way to grow will be through connection. I've learned more about pastoring through Facebook than 25 years of lectures, seminars, and conferences. In reality, I pastor a megachurch on Facebook. The last time I looked I had more than 1,400 friends.

Now I didn't set out to be a "mega" man on Facebook, it just happened (surprisingly) through intentional development of one community at a time. I found old friends, former students, personal family, brief acquaintances, and countless other folks through my associations and connection to their world. I just don't "friend" anyone either. I truly believe we have to have a connection. Perhaps we are blood-related. Perhaps I was a youth minister at their church once. Perhaps I was their professor for a class or season. Perhaps I led a workshop in their area. Perhaps we went to high school together.

Regardless of the reason, with 99.9 percent of my Facebook friends I've probably shared a handshake, a meal, a moment, or some type of social community. Perhaps that includes *you!*

Facebook is a cultural example for how smaller church youth ministries can create electrifying connections and engaging community. In 2009, Facebook was the number one social media site with more than 250 million users.[2] It's the largest mall, church, school, and reunion in the world, but it didn't start out to be "mega." It wasn't the brainchild of some computer expert in Silicon Valley. No, the creator of Facebook was a heartbroken college sophomore named Mark Zuckerberg. He had just lost his girlfriend, his life was a mess, and he needed an outlet. He knew he wasn't alone and so in 2004 Zuckerberg created "The Facebook" to fill a social need within his Harvard campus for better student community. "Everyone's been talking a lot about a universal face book within Harvard," Zuckerberg told his school newspaper. "I think it's kind of silly that it would take the university a couple of years to get around to it. I can do it better than they can, and I can do it in a week."[3] He was right.

[2]en.wikipedia.org/wiki/Facebook
[3]thecrimson.com/article.aspx?ref=357292

Literally overnight his idea had spread to thousands of Harvard students and continued to pick up steam when he expanded it to other Ivy League schools. In less than six months "The Facebook" reached tens of thousands of college kids. So Zuckerman moved his dorm room company to Palo Alto, California, and incorporated. He dropped the "the" and further expanded Facebook to all colleges and universities. In 2005, he launched a high school version that quickly spread nationally and a year later Facebook finally was available to anyone over 13. The rest is social networking history.

The appeal of Facebook is simple: Create connection and forge community around interests, hobbies, political persuasions, memorable events, past acquaintances, business opportunities, and dozens of other groups, "fan" pages, and games. For all the criticism—and there's plenty—Facebook has led the pack in social networking. Unlike Twitter, MySpace, and YouTube, on Facebook you only "friend" people you want and can actually "de-friend" them later if you change your mind. Facebook puts you in control of the people you allow into your life. You have the power over what people view about you; consequently, Facebook remains one of the safer social networking sites for personal content display.

What you can't control is what others post about you. That's the messy side of community and open-source multi-verse culture. If one of your "friends" decides to upload a hideous better-left-buried photo of you from high school, there's not much you can do about it (except personally plead for your friend to remove it). What's worse? How you react may exacerbate the situation. The more you gripe about the dreadful photo on your "friend's wall" the worse it gets, as your statements get posted into other feeds, including dozens of people who don't even know you.

Suddenly a small insignificant photo, probably only enjoyed by a few (with you groaning about it) becomes flashed and promoted wildly. This is the viral subversive nature of social networking sites.

Emerging generations don't seem to mind this type of openness. In fact, radical transparency is a shared value in social networking. Radical transparency is unfettered honesty in a post, gutsy status updates, off-color video uploads, edgy and inappropriate photos, and profane statements about personal political views. But that still doesn't eliminate social consequence.

If you push the envelope too much you'll get the boot. The community (your friends) set the social norms and if you wear out your welcome it's adios. At Facebook you won't necessarily know who "de-friended" or why. All you know is your "friend" number is falling (which is a good indication that you're more than a little socially unacceptable!). Of course, common values and interests drive most friend lists so "de-friending" someone is rare and usually happens more out of conflict. We tend to tolerate obnoxious friends because what we hold in common is of greater value than individual eyesores.

DON'T COUNT PEOPLE, MAKE PEOPLE COUNT

If this sounds like a smaller church, you got the picture.

The smaller church looks like a living Facebook. It's a collection of flawed friends who have connected and built a faith community. It's why *small is tall*. It's also why growth is only one relationship away. After all, if true transparency is valued, deep community is cherished, and engaging connections are pursued, then you won't stay "small" long.

You'll grow in influence and "tall" impact.

But here's the catch: *It might not be in numbers.*

In the Newtonian church, numbers counted for everything. It was all about production and results (converts, budgets, attendances, staff, facilities). Big was better and success was linked to size. The Newtonian church (denomination) controlled its marketing strategies, worship experiences, membership rolls, and pastoral staff. But in the emerging 21C church, numbers are relative. They're not absolute indicators of success.

In fact, you can be the biggest on the block and be a failure when compared to smaller congregations that maximize their community in greater percentages. This doesn't mean numbers aren't important. They do matter but only in relationship to the community.

Many smaller churches and smaller church youth ministries struggle to grow because of where they are planted. Although there are notable exceptions, most congregations are limited by the population of their area. If you live in a rural context, you also have resource limitations. But instead of focusing upon the limits, look beyond to the license.

Let's get back to Facebook. I'll confess that sometimes I feel good about how many "friends" I might have at the site and sometimes when I see my friend list take a dive, I wonder who it is and why they left. But I must confess that as much as I like every one of my friends, this growing friend list forced changes in how I live on Facebook. For example, I turned off the chat function. It's not a big deal with a dozen friends, but when you have hundreds it can be a nuisance. I don't "play" like I used to either. I block all the game invites or suffer through dozens of new requests every day.

"*The Christian tradition is teamwork-obsessed. The doctrine of creation trumpets a God who shares creative power with us, who insists we be co-conspirators in our own story, collaborators in our emergence. The doctrine of redemption is the universe's story of pulsating and materializing relationships. The very doctrine of the Trinity is based on a relational God living in community both within and without.*"

—Leonard Sweet, futurist and author *AquaChurch: Essential Leadership Arts for Piloting Your Church in Today's Fluid Culture*

Because I have so many friends my "home feed" is constantly changing with new status updates, and that means I miss out on 80 percent of what's going on in my friends' lives. In some ways I miss being "small" and tightly connected to only a few.

The advantage for smaller youth ministries to develop lasting community is unparalleled and largely unrealized. You can create connections that larger churches can only dream of crafting. You can engage and interact with students on a level megachurches cannot. You can develop deep relationships and lifelong friendships that struggle to root within larger contexts.

You see, the larger you get as a youth ministry, the more you have to organize and distance yourself from the students. You can't personally touch or reach every teenager. You don't get to "play" like you used to (without being criticized for having favorites). You have to block invitations to school plays, games, concerts, and other student activities because you don't have time to do them all. And you start to lose inside information and drop outside the loop. You don't know about everything that's happening in your students' lives.

It's a blessing to grow big, but it's also a burden.

It's why larger churches tend to be more mechanistic and program-centered rather than humane and person-centered. It's not that they don't care about kids (they do) but size changes the system. In the smaller church youth ministry our smallness is strength.

It's not hard to lose the programmed, impersonal, organized, traditional approach to youth ministry, especially in the smaller church. All you have to do is return to your original DNA. Get back to family.

Make a U-Turn and rediscover the joy of community and congregation. When you silo your youth ministry and separate it from the other age groups, you risk relationships. Sure, it may look good on the surface and plenty of adults (especially church leaders living in the old paradigm) will applaud you, but your goal isn't a "program"—it's developing mature followers of Christ.

And that happens within community. It takes a church to raise a teenager.

So what you need to do is F.A.C.E.B.O.O.K. and wire your youth ministry to reflect these dynamic forces.

FAMILY FOCUS

In youth ministry we talk a lot of good stuff about being family-centered and family-focused, but our programming betrays our words. If most of your youth ministry involves separating teenagers from their parents, then you're not family-focused. Smaller churches have a deep advantage on this point because we're largely patriarchal and matriarchal in nature anyway, meaning there are a few families that control the congregation.

It's part of our DNA. Smaller congregations are simply a collection of families seeking God and following Jesus. And when we siphon and separate kids from parents we operate not only against biblical principle but cultural desire.

ALL-CHURCH EVENTS

The professionalization of youth ministry in the 1980s and the emergence of youth ministry as a "silo" (separate entity within the church) had significant consequence on whole-congregational events.

I grew up in a church without a youth pastor, but that doesn't mean we were without a youth ministry. In fact, by all measures, the youth ministry in that small church of 90 was immeasurable, because dozens of young men and women are active leaders in their churches to this day. What did that little church do differently? We had a weekly meeting, usually in someone's home, but the greatest difference was our all-church perspective. We hung out together.

Once a month we enjoyed an all-church fellowship dinner after Sunday services. It was rare for anyone to skip and common for everyone to stay for several hours—playing pingpong or football, and talking. We brought in the New Year together with a film festival and game night. We had a Valentine's Day banquet, Easter sunrise service, Memorial Day lake trip, Fourth of July fireworks, Labor Day family camp, Thanksgiving dinner, and Christmas party. These were whole family events. All welcome. Nobody catered the meals either. Each family brought a little something. Many hands made light work.

Smaller church youth ministries can lead the church back to being an "all-church" community again. There are a few cultural holidays that are can't-miss opportunities for the congregation to gather: Super Bowl Sunday, New Year's Eve, Fourth of July, and Halloween. Ironically, those outside the church use all of these "holy-days" to connect, converse, and congregate.

Why should the church miss all the fun?

COMMUNITY AND CULTURE

Of course, all-church events can easily become all-community opportunities, but it's not enough to build community within a congregation—we must also move outside. Literally. When we focus on our neighbors, we lose sight of ourselves. Many adolescents are keenly aware of community need. The problem is they don't know how to pull off the vision. Imagine the potential your church could enjoy if teenagers were allowed to lead.

We also need to introduce teenagers to the world. By 2050, many current minorities (Asian, Hispanic, African-American) will comprise the majority in U.S. population. The "white captivity" of the church in western culture is fading as new tribes, ethnic groups, and races influence what it means to be the church in a multicultural society. Your adolescents are rubbing shoulders with Muslims, Buddhists, Hindus, Jews, and every flavor of Christian from Catholic to Pentecostal.

Our faith is forged within community. When we limit our experiences to a single, narrow perspective (white, black, brown, yellow, orange, or blue), we steal opportunities to grow, influence, and change.

EXPERIENTIAL LEARNING

It's been well said that people believe what they do more than do what they believe. Many teenagers believe going to church is a good thing but fewer and fewer do it. Yet adolescents who are deeply tied to a youth group and church community will vociferously defend the value of regular attendance. Why? It's because they believe what they *do*.

Experiential learning is relationally rooted. It happens best within the context of a community. But it's not easy or simple or always clear. Many teachers dismiss experiential learning because they can't control it. Exactly. A common experience might inspire countless feelings, attitudes, and conversations. We experience things through the frame we've inherited. That's what makes it messy. You need others to help you discern, sort, evaluate, apply, and understand what you've experienced. You need mentors who'll safely help you to grow through feelings that may betray or bar.

Because we'll talk more about experiential learning in the next chapter, we'll save the juicy stuff for later.

BRANDING

If you could communicate your youth ministry in three words, what would they be? Why? And would your students agree with your answer?

In 21C culture the brand belongs to the people.

The power of marketing explodes through social advertising, blogs, posts, comments, praise, and other kudos. It didn't used to be this way. Even a few short years ago the brand belonged to the company. The organization, business, church, or school controlled its brand (many educational institutions still work this way), but with the emergence of Web 2.0 the brand is now hyper-connective and communal.

Who we are is how the community *feels* about us—even if they're dead wrong.

So it doesn't matter how you brand yourself, if your consumers (parents, teenagers, church leaders) disagree you're essentially toast.

In old school youth ministry, the goal was "majority rule." If most parents were on board, that was good enough. If most teenagers were coming, that was success. If most church leaders approved, the proposal passed. But in 21C culture, the disappointed and disgusted minority can create quite a ruckus. One e-mail, one Facebook status update, or one text message can balloon into a zeppelin of conflict and controversy. Viral negativity is a youth ministry's worst nightmare.

That's the power of a social brand. It's not all about you but about youth. It's not me but we—which is "me" turned upside down.

ONLINE [SOCIAL NETWORKING] PRESENCE

Social marketing happens virally through relational community. It's how something small (like an idea, YouTube video, post, or group) can explode into a major presence. It's what makes a Susan Boyle a global celebrity.

Twenty-first century youth ministry will exploit social networks to expand influence with teenagers in their community. Maybe in the future it won't be Facebook or YouTube, though these two currently are super-brands within social networks, but it will be *something*. Emerging culture is (and will continue to be) socially connected via Web portals. If the church fails to adopt these technological opportunities it's akin to taking a mission trip to a foreign land and not learning the language, eating the cuisine, or enjoying the native culture.

Social networks are the new malls. You've heard of Minneapolis' Mall of America? Facebook is the Mall of the *World*. It's where kids currently congregate to socialize.

Are you kidding me? It's where adults currently congregate! I tap into my FB at the office and always find at least 40 of my adult friends online during the workday. (Maybe I shouldn't have said that out loud.)

Of course, this might not even be true in six months so don't build a bungalow at Facebook—erect a tent. In 21C culture we're nomadic in nature and just as the Israelites wandered the desert with a portable tabernacle, so must we. God is on the move and we can't contain him in a temple or website or time. Many youth ministries carved a MySpace presence in the early 21st century only to find by 2009 that MySpace was no longer the social networking darling.

Twitter is another popular social network, but its popularity is already trending downward, as people "tweet" to Twitter (via Facebook, mobile devices, Ping, and so on) but don't actually go to the website. In youth ministry, Twitter has even less value and has found few fans among the under-18 crowd. Teenagers text but don't tweet.

I'm way over 18 and even I'm already over Twitter.

Nevertheless, social networking reveals how the small can be tall!

OPTIMIZED MINISTRY

We can all hope that the era of the lone ranger youth pastor is over. This concept is both unbiblical (every believer is a minister) and culturally out of step.

Smaller church youth ministries can easily lead the charge to restore teenagers as leaders in the church of today, not just tomorrow.

I call it turbo-charged ministry.

It's simply an intentional commitment to no longer do youth ministry in isolation. Optimized ministry recognizes every ministry moment as a teachable leadership opportunity.

Develop a posse mentality where everywhere you are working, there's a group of kids tagging along.

This is how Jesus did ministry.

His disciples were in a continual community and with rare exception were privy to river healings, cemetery exorcisms, Galilee boat rides, roadside executions, feasts with Pharisees, and synagogue lectures. Of course, we could argue these were first-century adults not 21st century adolescents—and that's fine—but it's also missing the point. Many of Jesus' disciples were children and teenagers, too (who followed with their folks), whether a boy with fish sandwiches or little children.

Everywhere Jesus ventured he created a ministry culture by involving crowds in his business. He traveled with 12 and taught thousands, he communed with the religious and irreligious, and he spent more time in the field than behind a lectern.

Everywhere Jesus traveled he took his followers. Youth ministry doesn't happen in a vacuum. We are a collection of experiences emerging from community.

He has enabled us to be ministers of his new covenant. This is a covenant not of written laws, but of the Spirit. The old written covenant ends in death; but under the new covenant, the Spirit gives life (2 Corinthians 3:6 NLT).

KITCHEN MEETINGS

Food is the way to a man's heart—and most women's hearts too.

So why not create community around meals and host table conferences?

It doesn't matter what type of meeting—involve food and you'll attract a crowd. In the smaller church youth ministry we have countless opportunities to explore meeting meals, and these connections don't necessarily have to happen in a home either, but a restaurant, a coffee shop, or even a local food festival.

Kitchen meetings are excellent community builders. Food has a way of opening our hearts to share, connect, and relate. Maybe that's why Jesus did his best ministry around a meal. He understood the power of the fork!

In case you missed it, see the meal-planning event at the end of Chapter 6.

If you've paid attention, very few of these eight dynamics happen at a church or are limited by space and time. In 21C culture we operate 24/7/365. Maybe the best meeting time for your teenagers isn't Wednesday at 7 p.m. but Friday at 6 a.m. Maybe the optimum spot for volunteers to gather is a coffee shop at 4 p.m. on Tuesdays.

I just had a conference call at midnight last night!

And if you fold in social networking and online portals the sky is the limit for connection, communication, and community. A Bible study conversation can last all week. A brainstorming session on summer events can happen across several days.

Finally, don't forget the opportunities to grow yourself as a leader. Follow wise sages at Twitter. Watch YouTube training videos or register for iTunes podcasts on youth ministry.

In an open-source, fluid, multi-verse culture, it will be messy and mistakes happen naturally. But that's what keeps us all real and relevant.

Smaller church youth ministries must invite connection, introduce conversation, and initiate community. The world has changed, from the smallest sub-atom to the largest mega-structure. It's no longer one size fits all. We can't program for the masses. We can't box God and confine Christ to a curriculum.

The success of our brand will be linked to the depth of community we create. For it's in our friendships that faith solidifies, even if only two or three gather in his name.

We *are* who we are.

JOIN RICK ON FACEBOOK!

Just search for "Leading From the Edge Training, Workshops, and Consultations." You'll receive daily feeds, links, quotes, and videos on cultural changes that impact church, business, education, and home. It's like a college class except tuition-free. I'm also on Twitter and LinkedIn!

Steph's 2 Cents

Wow! Rick has hit the mark on this longtime church-size sore spot. Age-level ministry fans on one side and intergenerational on the other. Sometimes small churches are looked down upon for their "one-school room" approach to outreach event planning as if they can't keep up with the big (church) dogs. Don't listen to the nay-saying tongue cluckers. Your ministry outreach will succeed if you do what you can and do it well.

I'm here to tell you that the family approach to youth ministry is one of the BEST tools a smaller church has in its toolbox. Family-based youth and children's ministry is alive, well, and extremely effective.

My church does it all the time and I bet yours does, too.

Just in case your smaller church needs a refresher course in intergenerational outreach ideas, here's a list of community builders that can span your members' age scope. Since I'm a holiday fan, I've designed these around favorite family days of the year.

Christmas Caroling Party

Have the youth do the marketing and the children make Christmas cards to leave at each door. Ask older folks to provide the "after party" cookies and hot chocolate. Parents do the driving and everybody sings!

Church-wide Christmas Dinner

Who doesn't love a children's Christmas program? It brings back warm fuzzy thoughts for teenagers up to great-grandmas. So have your kids put on a program or play. Anything they do would be appreciated. They have the adorable factor going for them. Youth are always looking for a way to earn trip money so let them do the dinner as a fundraiser. Have a "decorate a table" contest for the women of the church and ask the men to do the setup and cleanup. Have your older folks sell the tickets. There's your party!

Double Egg Hunt

Most of us are already doing egg hunts, right? Here's a great intergenerational twist my mom's little country church does every year. While the older adults are hiding Easter eggs for the kids, the kids are hidings eggs for the older adults in another part of the church! The eggs for the "more mature" members hold hard candies, bookmarks, clips, and so on. After each group hunts for their eggs, they all meet in the middle to open their treasures, make crafts, and snack! Fun, huh?

Family Movie Nights

We're doing one a month and each one is sponsored by a different age group or has a different purpose. For example, our November movie event is "turkey hot dog" night and includes a showing of "A Charlie Brown Thanksgiving." For Christmas, the youth are showing "The Polar Express" a week before Christmas for the kids so Mom and Dad can squeeze in some "alone time" shopping. Easy to do! (Side note: The tradeoff for my youth on their December Parent's Night Out is that they talked me into a Christmas Lock-out after the wee ones go home. I'm such a sap even after all these years.)

Trunk or Treat

Kids are going to trick-or-treat whether we agree with the philosophy of Halloween or not. So let's use it as a way to reach out to the families around our churches. This idea is one that the older folks will love since many of them miss the days of costumed kids. Advertise your event as a two-hour time frame on Halloween. That night, have drivers line up their cars in your church parking lot, trunk side out. Ask the adults to bring Halloween candy and decorations for their trunk. Pop the trunk, decorate, and watch the kids flock to your church. Add a story-telling time of The Pumpkin Patch Parable and you've shared the Gospel.

Annual Pumpkin Patch

If you're in a smaller church, a pumpkin patch won't succeed unless everyone works together. It takes everyone in my church to make this yearly church fundraiser happen. We moan and groan about it every year but we really love it. We even have a silly song our band made up and members start clamoring for it every September.

To make the patch work, the under-40 crowd unloads the pumpkins. The youth turn the pumpkins every few days. Adults in our church, mostly ladies, get together and bake pumpkin bread. The retired crowd works the day shifts, the parents work the night shifts, and the children make sure the hay gets spread everywhere! Even if your church doesn't need to do a patch for the money, I highly recommend it. (And what church doesn't need the money?)

Vacation Bible School

By its very nature, VBS is a community builder so make sure you're offering something for everyone! Use youth as assistant crew leaders; you could also tack on another hour each day with a study just for them. Always provide an adult class during VBS for the folks that aren't working the VBS. It's a great place to channel new parents who want to stay near their kids. Everyone attends the opening and closing together.

A Good Old-Fashioned Church Picnic

Do NOT sell this idea short! It's an oldie but a goody and there's a good reason. Churches have been doing this for years. Think about it: Everyone still has to eat, grilling out is still a family favorite, and baseball is still America's favorite pastime. Plan it and do it. Can you believe there are lots of kids who haven't had the privilege of this all-time church family favorite?

There are so many more ideas available like an Advent Wreath-making Event, Faith-Storytelling Night, Lenten Pretzel Baking, and more. Be intentional about building in God moments in each event. Get folks talking with one another. Involve everyone in hands-on ways and you'll see the unity in your community grow.

CHAPTER NINE ◎ CHA CHA SUNDAY SCHOOL

"If there is one overarching principle that defines what the new Web is, it's that we are building this thing together—one blog post, podcast, and mash-up after another. The Web is no longer about idly surfing and passively reading, listening, or watching. It's about peering: sharing, socializing, collaborating, and, most of all, creating within loosely connected communities."[1]
—Don Tapscott

"Video Killed the Radio Star"
—The Buggles

Have you learned to "ChaCha" yet?

You better step on it—and quick! Just like television forever changed radio's dominance, the Web is transforming how we teach and learn. ChaCha is just one of many emerging examples. Teenagers text this site for every answer under the sun. Billed as "ur mobile BFF" (your mobile best friend forever), ChaCha is as popular as Google for answering some of life's most difficult (and mundane) questions, especially when all you have is a cell phone. A simple text to "ChaCha" and in a matter of minutes you have the solution—or at least an answer, even if you don't like it. And when you travel to www.chacha.com you'll also get a read on the most popular topics pricking current culture, including how to kiss, what girls/boys like, how to know if you're pregnant, what's a good salary, and what's a Ouija board.

Perhaps the online encyclopedia Wikipedia is better known.

[1]Don Tapscott, *Wikinomics: How Mass Collaboration Changes Everything*, (New York: Penguin Books, 2006): 45

It's a collaborative resource created by millions of individuals and guided by an editorial board that confirms facts, checks sources, and flags entries as controversial or requiring more proof.

Wikipedia allows anonymous users to participate and change, alter, improve, and upload new content. Critics have long charged Wikipedia is open to abuse (what prevents anyone from writing anything?) but they miss the point. The Wiki community is constantly self-correcting misinformation—much of it with certifiable links to research, statistics, and hard evidence—and improving it. In some ways, it's more reliable—and certainly more current—than the encyclopedia you consulted for research back in high school.

In an open-source, fluid, multi-verse culture, the transmission of knowledge will be messy and mistakes will be part of the process. In a 21C culture, truth is limited to perspective and naturally biased or prejudiced. Every article and book, every professor and teacher, every lecture and lesson is naturally censored and controlled, creating natural distrust of information sources. You only get partial truth because all you receive is *their* perspective. For many younger generations, the Bible—not the original writings but the countless subsequent translations—is seen as flawed and framed by the interpreter's theological assumptions, Hebrew or Greek understanding, historical and cultural knowledge, and personal feelings. Even if you mastered Greek and could read the earliest manuscript for a biblical book you would still translate it through your own lens. Nobody is purely objective. We are what our environment has produced. Consequently, literary documents—especially ancient ones like the Bible—are suspicious, flawed, and open to skepticism.

For many church leaders and educators this doubt is dangerous. After all, the goal of Christian education for centuries has been *indoctrination*. During the Enlightenment, Christian education adopted cultural conventions and put God into a frame (systematic theology) and then taught the frame (via outline, syllabus, or curriculum). All other frames were labeled as flawed, weak, or even heretical. It was believed if you could control both subject and student, censoring information that's contradictory, confusing, or conflicting, then you would develop a disciple without doubt. Knowledge was power and the pinnacle of understanding was intellectualism. Therefore, learning methods like the lecture, chalkboard, handout, and later video/film were popular strategies for cramming content and force-feeding information. Objective testing (true/false, short answer, fill-in-the-blank) evaluated the teaching process. If students could regurgitate the information ("Will this be on the test?") they were then validated as having learned the content.

In a 21C culture, a massive amount of knowledge is only a mouse click away. You don't need a professor or teacher to tell you stuff anymore. Anybody who learns to use Google may access information once reserved only for the sage and scholar. The problem is multiple streams of information create countless contradictions, perspectives, differences, and ideas. Interactive media such as Facebook, YouTube, and Wikipedia allow individuals to offer their own viewpoints, opinions, and skewed facts. Consequently, anyone who surfs for information starts with a natural distrust and healthy skepticism. Emerging educators recognize today's learners won't blindly swallow knowledge.

"We have entire industries and institutions built on the fact that the paper order severely limits how things can be organized... educational curricula...[are] based on the assumption that... we need experts to go through information, ideas, and knowledge and put them neatly away. But now we... anyone...can do it ourselves and, more significantly, do it together..."

—David Weinberger, technologist and author *Everything is Miscellaneous: The Power of the New Digital Disorder*

Are you sure, Rick? Because I see media's subjective opinions influencing fiction into "fact" and not always truthful.

Therefore, emerging methods like conversation, debate, group projects, or opportunities to create (PowerPoint, website, art, music, writing) are infinitely more potent tools. It's not about what you know as much as *why* you know it. Critical thinking is the buzzword. Teachers don't force-feed knowledge but facilitate learning. Educators create community in order to foster dialogue, learning, and life change.

CREATING WE...

A more organic approach to Christian education that focuses on *influence* not indoctrination is proving more appealing to 21C culture. It doesn't mean truth isn't taught, but rather that truth is lived first. Truth arises out of an active community and is intimately tied to the stories of a person, a group, or a society.

In reality, there's a beauty and efficacy to communal learning as an avenue for the transference of knowledge and translation of truth. For thousands of years, what a culture "knew" was communicated through narratives. The Jewish Passover is a classic example, as are the four Gospels. It's also how the Jewish Talmud (instruction, learning) emerged in the fourth century B.C. Until enslaved by Babylonia, the Jews relied upon oral communication to transfer the stories, interpretations and doctrine of the Torah (Genesis, Exodus, Leviticus, Numbers, and Deuteronomy). In Jewish culture, rabbis memorized the Torah verbatim and used the Temple as a place for holy learning. However, when the Jews were taken captive, Jerusalem sacked, and the Temple destroyed, the importance of retaining Jewish values became infinitely more important.

In ancient cultures, few survived the overthrow by a foreign nation. Most commoners—aged, disabled, diseased, women, children—were slaughtered by the tens of thousands.

Of the survivors, many died in transit to their new alien colony, including a few by suicide. Only the best and brightest captives were even hauled into captivity, and many were dignitaries, royals, or upper class (and nearly all were adolescents). The goal was to mold these stellar youth into state slaves and political peacekeepers, liaisons, and stewards. Part of the cultural indoctrination process involved a name change, plus force-feeding new social and cultural norms (food, dress, religious customs). The goal was to brainwash allegiance to a new king. Failure to comply was met with swift and certain death (lions' dens and fiery furnaces).

Consequently, as this transported Jewish culture learned to operate within foreign captivity, they especially relied upon the rabbis to retain their heritage, culture, and faith. These influential rabbis developed sayings, offered interpretations, shared applications and legal opinions (a.k.a. Mishnah) to the Law (Torah) and enabled Jews to remain culturally "Jewish." Initially, these teachings were strictly oral—and the result of communal academic debate and dialogue. However, after generations of Jewish captivity and history, the need for a permanent record emerged. Two rabbis—Rav Muna and Rav Yossi—compiled the Talmud. As time passed the Talmud surfaced as the "Jewish Wikipedia" for practical faith and grew in size as new generations of rabbis added commentary. In conservative Judaism, the Talmud remains authoritative and a living document of faith. It's also an example of how community guides and guards the revelation of Truth.

The Talmud is a scholarly work but also very practical; it's rooted in past revelation but relevant to current culture; it's a fluid work of community yet focused upon individual faith.

The goal of the Talmud was to influence interpretation and opinion among the people. Yes, it indoctrinated to a degree but the humanness of perspective allowed it to breathe and move. The Talmud was never meant to be authoritative, a rule or law, but affirmative of the Law. It was a cultural commentary on God's guidelines for life as it played out in a particular time, place, or situation.

Ironically, most smaller churches have unwritten "talmuds" for faith and practice already in existence. These are interpretations of biblical statements, personal opinions, and expansive explanations for church by-laws. These ecclesiastical "talmuds" mark where a church has been, what it is, and where it's going. They're the living oral traditions that make a church a unique community. They're the stories that define, the doctrines that frame, and the opinions that guide and guard.

Great point, Rick. Understanding what's at the DNA of your church's belief system is a pivotal point of helping productive learning among your people.

Consequently, every church educates *differently*. We may have similar statements of faith, but in reality, a congregation is a community of metanarratives, stories, experiences, and interpretations about life, tradition, and Scripture. The smaller (and older) the church the more obvious, rigid, and communicated these "talmuds of tradition" become. A long history creates countless communal changes, tweaks, corrections, and deletions to "who we are" as a church.

Consequently, Christian education isn't in a box or a building or a program. It's not about indoctrination, as much as influence.

Our goal isn't to produce theological robots but faithful Christians. Therefore, Christian education—the attraction, assimilation, and preparation of people into Christ's body, the church—is naturally messy, communal, oral, and impacted by our congregational narrative. Think about your church's pet doctrines and rituals: Sinner's prayer? Confirmation? Baptism? Confession? Holiday traditions? Order of service? Sermon? Or maybe some of your church's unwritten rules like no food in the sanctuary, no running in the building, no playing in the baptismal water, or no talking in church? Where do we get these faith guidelines? Certainly some have biblical statements (evangelism, baptism) but most emerged from community interpretation (Baptist, Catholic, Methodist, Presbyterian, non-denominational) and experience (service/worship preferences, facility rules, and holiday rituals).

That's why converting a portion of the sanctuary at my church into a Coffee Café was such a struggle for some of the older members of my church. In their well-established faith guidelines, they see sitting with a cup of coffee during worship as disrespectful to God. They worked it out by just not looking over toward that direction.

Christian education, then, is influence via both indoctrination and assimilation. It's introducing the "faith" (as interpreted and passed down through denominational heritage) as well as integrating "traditions" (as created by the local church community over the years) into the hearts and minds of each person. Christian education happens all the time and it's not confined to Sunday school or small group Bible studies.

When a sermon is preached, that's Christian education. When we're taught how to worship "in spirit and truth," that's Christian education. When we walk into the building, it educates us through signage, icons, pictures, paintings, and photos.

Every person helps educate another person in the faith—intentionally or unintentionally. Every person is a teacher, and we either propel or repel faith in others.

We are a community of scholars, pastors, teachers, and mentors who create a living "ecclesiastical talmud" for our congregation to explain mysteries, communicate history, outline rituals, interpret biblical statements, and offer opinions of faith and practice. The power of the smaller church is that more people can participate in this communal experience. The larger the church the more such roles are diffused to leaders, professional clergy, or in-house scholars. The smaller congregation truly operates within a rabbinic role to "wiki" a community understanding and practice.

CREATING WII...

In 21C culture, everybody plays ball. It's not a spectator sport. Have you noticed the "Wii" video game phenomenon? Why do they call it "Wii?" Perhaps because you need a "we" to truly play the video games as intended. Maybe it's because it's a hoot to play (Whee!). Or perhaps as one clever online blogger noted it's "wireless, interactive, intelligent" technology.[2] Regardless of the reason, Wii video gaming has dominated the market. It has discovered how to "wiki" (collaborative gaming) and "ChaCha" (intelligent tech) to the top.

[2]http://uk.answers.yahoo.com/question/index?qid=20061207065507AAN32h2

> "There's nothing like watching teens respond to stories when we tell them with life and color. But I also believe that we need to do more. What we need in our stories is a solid theology… We should be doing what I call 'theo-topical' preaching—where the messages are designed to help shape kids' theological grids and force them to think… Postmodern teens are starving for this."
>
> —Dan Kimball, pastor and author (Quoted by Tony Jones in *Postmodern Youth Ministry*)

And so must Christian education within the smaller church.

Your youth ministry is ground zero for future faith. If the children that arrive in middle school ministry later graduate biblically anorexic, spiritually comatose, or flat-lined in their faith, it's *our* fault.

We have a deep responsibility to introduce faith, integrate spirituality, initiate growth, and instill a biblical worldview—not for a few moments in high school but for a lifetime. It's a big job, and in 21C culture it's gotten a lot easier if we choose to "ChaCha" (bite-size answers), "wiki" (collaborative learning), and foster the "Wii" in biblical teaching (edutainment).

I've been privileged to teach adolescents Scripture for well over a quarter century, and I'm excited about what the future holds for church education and biblical learning. The smaller church and its youth ministries are certainly primed for success, as learning communities in the future will go W-I-I with advantage to the small!

WIRELESS LEARNING

Cyber communication has flattened hierarchies and opened multiple streams for information to flow. In the future, learning technologies will expand our ability to teach from a distance, and by 2020 many futurists believe the end of "brick and mortar" education may be in sight. Why go to a place at a certain time when you can time-shift and space-shift your learning to your schedule? Online learning happens 24/7/365 and will continue to explode in popularity.

The really good news? Most of it will be *free*. That's right—nada, zip, gratis!

It's already happening.

Major universities post professor lectures, PowerPoint presentations, videos, and other learning resources for anyone to access. Google is near completion of a digitized book collection that will create the largest library in the world.

You'll be able to research original sources, founding documents, statistical research, and books by influential thinkers with just a mouse click. If you go to iTunes you'll find "iTunes U"—a depository of content from some of our world's greatest thinkers. Or go to TED.com and connect to a complementary classroom of cultural influencers.

Church education needs to explore wireless opportunities, and smaller churches are a perfect venue for creating connection and community. Perhaps it's an e-Sunday school or e-Bible study. Perhaps social media can be used to foster learning and teach biblical concepts beyond the walls of a church. Smaller congregations, with their ability to correct, change, and carve new courses of action, possess a decided edge in online Christian education and spiritual e-learning. And dollar for dollar, it's also far less expensive than conventional curriculum.

INTERACTIVE LEARNING

Social media have created a connective community that allows individuals to post and upload content. This has flattened authority and innovated how we think about information. For the past several centuries, learning was passive, rote, and non-participatory, but in a Web world everybody can be a teacher, publisher, filmmaker, or artist.

YouTube and Facebook, particularly, are rooted in relational interaction and member participation. Auction giant eBay and retail Goliath Amazon use buyer feedback to create integrity and foster sales. It used to be a company could control how its brand was produced and promoted but no more.

Buyers now own the companies, and viral feedback—both positive and negative—can make or break a sale and, eventually, a whole company.

In a Web world everybody's talking and everyone's listening.

Take Twitter, the 140-word micro-blog that's helping shape how we interact and communicate. Twitter is little more than bumper sticker education. It's knowledge reduction—whether personal, professional, academic, or trivial—into bite-size nuggets. A tweet is like shouting at a busy mall on a Saturday night. It's not the most effective communication tool, but with volume comes voice. Because only a few people (a.k.a. "followers") will hear or read your insight or idea, it requires either multiple tweeting to reach more individuals or enlarging your "following" for deeper influence. Twitter encourages brevity, clarity, and introspection. Those with Twitter ears to hear may reply or respond, producing a relational loop. Knowledge is no longer static or one-way information to be translated, digested, and regurgitated on some test, project, or evaluation tool. Knowledge isn't contained to a billboard, bumper sticker, or PowerPoint slide.

In 21C culture, knowledge is organic and breathes. It possesses life and grows, attaches, confronts, and reveals itself. Knowledge has a heartbeat, legs, hands, eyes, ears, nose, and mouth. Knowledge is wired for discussion through relationship, interaction, and community.

"We make a big teaching blunder when we think more is better. We try to cram so much into our people's noggins that they haven't a clue what's essential and what isn't. In fact, when we throw them so many balls to juggle, they wind up dropping them all."

—Thom and Joani Schultz, founds of Group Publishing *Why Nobody Learns Much of Anything at Church (And How to Fix It)*

What we know rises from *whom* we know (and trust).

Consequently, smaller churches that develop relationships and foster community will discover their teenagers are keenly aware and open to follow Christ. The advantage to a smaller size is the opportunity to be more interactive. It's human nature to become more passive in larger learning environments. Think about a lecture hall with 50, 100, or 500 students. It's not designed for dialogue—nor is that encouraged. The "content dump" is the strategy of choice and rarely will it elicit participation, unless the professor pauses for scheduled periods of discussion (which, depending on class size, are highly regulated through time). However, small groups of quads, trios, and even pairs naturally spark interaction. It's more of a coffeehouse experience where kindred souls share about life and faith.

INTELLIGENT LEARNING

The most important cognitive skill in 21C culture is critical thinking. The ability to understand, apply, analyze, synthesize, and evaluate knowledge in order to cultivate useful value will be as important as reading, writing, or 'rithmetic. The amount of information flying around us every day is mind-boggling. Thirty years ago, we watched three major news networks, listened to a solitary radio station (for hourly news updates) and mostly read a single locally published newspaper. Today, we have CNN, HLN, Fox News, Fox Business, MSNBC, CNBC, MTV News, The Weather Channel, and Current (to name only a few news outlets), plus Internet radio, XM, DIRECTV, Dish Network, USA Today, Reuters, Drudge Report, and countless blogs, podcasts, Facebook posts, and tweets. Information is now wider, deeper, and far more accessible.

Consequently, there are two identical and contrary errors that can emerge in an information-soaked culture. One is to rely solely upon a few favored single sources (which produces ignorance) or to accept every info-nugget from every source without critical examination (which produces superficiality).

Either mistake leads to a stilted worldview, bias, prejudice, and misunderstanding and opens a person to follow fanciful whims, cult personalities, or poor tastes.

Intelligent learning in 21C culture will equip people of all ages, particularly adolescents, to develop critical thinking skills. Benjamin Bloom outlines this process in his taxonomy for cognitive objectives.[3] I've further reduced them into the three "R"s: Recall, Reproduce, Reinvent.

In the recall stage, Bloom states knowledge is initially remembered and understood. On the journey to critical thinking, we begin by memorizing and comprehending information (translation, interpretation). In church education, this is highly emphasized, especially within children's ministry. However, it's also a common goal in adolescent and adult Sunday schools, Bible studies, discipleship, Bible college, and seminary education. *Remember the facts and what they're about. Spit it back out on a test and you pass.*

But that's just the beginning to critical thinking. The second stage is the ability to reproduce knowledge through application and analysis. Bloom argued knowledge now needed hands and feet, for when we make facts move we can then analyze their strengths and weaknesses. We can judge good and bad, deduct inferences, and produce generalizations.

"A human brain is only 38 percent developed at birth. All other mammals are 98 percent developed at birth. To be a human being is to be a continuous learner… Today's out-of-the-box breakthrough can become tomorrow's out-of-date antique faster than you can say 'eight-track.' The top of the class today will not be the of the class six months from now without an all-time learning culture."

—Leonard Sweet, futurist and author
AquaChurch: Essential Leadership Arts for Piloting Your Church in Today's Fluid Culture

---

[3]http://en.wikipedia.org/wiki/Taxonomy_of_Educational_Objectives

Tragically, very little church education currently expands beyond basic life application, mostly because we attempt to mass-produce disciples (via sermons, lectures, lessons) when this stage requires a personal touch through relational mentoring.

The final step to critical thinking is reinvention or as Bloom stated, synthesis and evaluation. These higher-order cognitive skills make knowledge sing its own tune. Facts aren't just facts.

They have history, breath, variety, and voice. The ability to think critically means you have a wide grasp of knowledge about a subject and understand the factors, contradictions, beauties, and conflicts to offer an "educated" opinion on the matter. The problem is few people get to this level of thinking and most are woefully content to remain blissfully ignorant.

And yet in an information age, ignorance is a poor excuse and a dangerous path. Smaller church youth ministries possess a special opportunity to teach critical thinking. The lower numbers allow us to deepen relational teaching and specialized mentoring. But it also means we need to continue to grow ourselves. We can't lead (or teach) where we've never been (or what we don't know).

HOW CHURCH EDUCATION IS CHANGING IN 21C

Traditional Religious Education	Emerging Religious Education
Learning rooted to time and space	Learning is 24/7/365, anywhere
Theology is a system (mechanized)	Theology is organic (relationship)
Focus upon content	Focus upon concepts
Intellectualism	Critical thinking
Mass communication	Individualized learning
Passive learning (lecture, video)	Experiential learning (sensory)
Learning is an answer/destination	Learning is questions/journey
Curriculum, Scope and Sequence, Hook/Book/Look/Took	Progressive dialogue, wiki-learning, life lessons
Individual Experience	Community Experience
Goal: Knowledge and Belief	Goal: Faith and Action
Paper-Driven: Teacher manuals, handouts, Bibles	Digitally-Driven: Downloads, Podcasts, e-Bibles
Teacher active, student passive	Student active, teacher passive

TEACHING REIMAGINED...

Let me also suggest we need to reimagine and reinvent what it means to "teach." Throughout the Renaissance and Enlightenment, the act of teaching became more hierarchal and passive in order to control the subject. Teachers moved away from relational models—as fostered within monasteries and early universities—toward communication models that focused more upon style and volume.

ATTRIBUTES OF LEARNER-CENTERED EDUCATION:

- *Built around the needs of the student, not the preferences or skill set of the teacher.*

- *Steadily evolves to meet the needs of its students, while a teacher-centered environment tends to be static and conventional in nature and content.*

- *Favors "depth" of learning over "breadth" of learning.*

- *Emphasizes experiential learning over memorization and repetition.*

- *Seeks to help students learn with and through one another.*

- *Emphasizes process over product.*

—Chris Folmsbee, author and youth ministry leader *A New Kind of Youth Ministry*

In the 18th and 19th centuries, debate shifted beyond a rhetorical device reserved for academics into public favor and popularity. Lecture became an art form, and communicators reduced subject matter to principles, points, and propositions. Words were all that mattered.

Consequently, the act of teaching was reduced to mass communication (one to many) and passivity. *Be quiet and listen. Stay in your seat. Focus your attention on me. Who's talking here?* As the Industrial Revolution reinvented production, it also impacted education. The one-room schoolhouse gave way to age-graded segregation and individual classrooms. Teachers became specialists, lecturers, and instructors. The use of standardized curriculum emerged and essentially treated every student the same. All of these educational innovations impacted church education. The greatest difference, however, was religious education delivered by volunteers—and many are ill prepared to use a curriculum, limited in biblical understanding, and busy.

The results have been dismal. If educational standards were equally applied to the church, many congregations would need to shut down their Sunday schools. We leave far too many students behind.

What we need is to reimagine Christian education, teaching, and learning. It's not about numbers, answers, pure doctrine, or creative curriculum, but about life change and spiritual growth. Too many congregations now rely upon a weekly sermon to mass manufacture disciples and cultivate faith. In reality, Christian education is individualized, messy, experiential, interactive, and narrative-driven.

Smaller churches can mentor adolescents deeper in the faith because less is more.

With a few kids we can personalize their faith and better aid the internalization of biblical concepts like grace, hope, love, sacrifice, service, and worship. When we teach a small class, we can use what Doug Pagitt terms "progressive dialogue" to communicate biblical truth.[4] Progressive dialogue focuses on the learner not the teacher and makes several assumptions about the communication process, many of which are central to teaching and learning:

- **Assumes God's truth resides in all people.** No one person has a corner on truth, including the teacher. Every person brings to the classroom "bits and pieces" of information that can be exhumed, examined, and evaluated. Naturally the younger you are, the less you bring to the table.

- **Provides a fuller understanding of the story.** Every individual is part of God's story ("his story"), and adolescents hunger to discover this truth. We deny teenagers their opportunity to join in God's narrative when we resort to lecture and passive learning. Theology is very organic in nature. Biblical stories are more than neat doctrinal points or propositions; they're outlandish, crazy, off-kilter revelations of how God worked and will continue to work even today. We don't water down truth by letting learners into the story—we actually strengthen God's story.

- **Shifts control to God.** The Spirit blows where he wants. The illusion, even delusion, of lecture-driven, passive learning is that it can be controlled. In reality, the nature of that control initiates a more sinister suggestion and promotes the idea the teacher is somehow God's spokesperson. I wonder how many times God looks down on a teacher and say, *"Hmmmm. Not what I meant"* or *"You can't be serious!"* or *"Wow. Aren't you something else?"*

[4]Doug Pagitt, *Preaching Re-Imagined* (Grand Rapids: Zondervan, 2005): 23.

- **Alters the community's relationship with the Bible.** Scriptures is a living and active sword (Hebrews 4:12). It's not a textbook (a common misconception in Bible colleges and Christian universities). It's not a book of principles, poetry, or platitudes. It's a dangerous tool. Like a scalpel it separates, slices, and severs our conscience. Like a sword it pricks our heart, punctures our biases, and penetrates our motives. It's not a safe book. It's not even a book! God's Word stands outside of scroll, paper, leather, or ink. It can't be contained within an e-book or limited by digitization either. God's Word moves, breathes, feels, looks, and listens. Our teenagers need to rediscover the majesty, power, and purpose of God's Word. We don't study it. It studies us.

- **Alters the relationship between pastor and congregation (or in our case, the teacher and class).** When we use dialogue not lecture to guide and guard our learning sessions, we flatten relationships and create a communal environment where everyone is a teacher and student (at the same time). Essentially, it's time teachers ceased to be the sage from the stage and become the guide from the side.

What will "progressive dialogue" look like in your church or youth group? In truth, no situation will be the same. Unlike a manufactured curriculum or lesson with a hook, book, look, and took, progressive dialogue focuses upon the student entering into the biblical story rather than the teacher exegeting and expounding upon it. And since every class is different, with varying understandings, experiences, biblical knowledge, and biases, no single pattern will emerge.

Does this mean you're not prepared to teach? Absolutely not! In fact, it really requires a teacher to pursue deeper preparation. Most of us view teaching like a slot machine. We fill ourselves up with quarters, and students, through the act of learning, pull our lever. Depending upon their need (pull), we deliver accordingly. We're just glorified, biblical cash cows that reward those who pursue to play the learning game. Of course, many won't pull the lever at all but what does that matter?

Actually I think it matters a lot—*especially* to God.

A far superior working metaphor for teaching is a spiritual GPS. I'll confess, I no longer fear getting lost or resist the urge to explore when I travel. Printed maps, even online, often failed miserably when plans changed due to traffic, construction, or situation. Recently I traveled to Southern California, and several spare hours before a flight provided opportunity to explore the beautiful coastal waters. I also wanted to enjoy another In-N-Out burger to accentuate my California experience. I simply typed in the restaurant and found several choices. I then entered a city on the coast and was on my way. Occasionally, I'd take a wrong turn or check out a side road, but my GPS remained a faithful guide. It didn't rebuke, criticize, or fail me. Rather it simply "recalculated" and provided another route.

This is 21C teaching in a snapshot. We don't lead the students—the students lead and we only "recalculate" when they miss the mark, incorrectly answer, or pursue a rabbit trail. Our work isn't to criticize as much as provide a fresh perspective, new insight, or better suggestion. We incarnate into a student's personal experience with God's Word, helping through life's traffic jams, crises, and accidents.

"To be a spiritual guide for youth and create a presence-centered youth ministry means youth workers must live, minister, guide, lead, and mentor out of the wholeness of their souls...a spiritual guide for youth is infected, consumed, and fixated with Jesus."

—Mike King, author and youth ministry organization leader *Presence-Centered Youth Ministry*

A GPS is only as good as its current map upgrade, and so are you. We need to continually learn to improve our skill, understanding, theology, and communication. We need to know where a student lives (culturally awareness and exegesis) so we can create spiritual maps to destinations that bring peace, hope, grace, and love. A GPS doesn't dump more than what you need to know. It continually reveals streets, stores, restaurants, and points of interest to enhance the path. Similarly, a master teacher lines lessons with creative stories, video clips, experiential activities, and rest stops for dialogue. A GPS isn't intimidated when I drive off the beaten path and you shouldn't be intimidated either. I love to teach this way! For me, it makes every class an adventure. It's not about me at all, but about my ability to transport my students to experience the best of anywhere they want to go.

We live in a world that's constantly changing and a culture that produces knowledge at rates and volumes unheard in history. It's a wiki world that loves to ChaCha (short but right answers). The smaller congregation inherently owns an opportunity to restore Christian education, teaching, and learning to a place of power and purpose. Like the captive Jews in Babylon we must transfer our biblical culture, lifestyle, stories, and doctrines to the students. We are literally creating a Talmud of Truth.

Smaller youth ministries own decided edges in relational learning and communal teaching strategies, but the spoils go to those who properly prepare to teach and not just dump knowledge.

After all, as an ancient proverb states: *To teach is to learn…twice.*

Steph's 2 Cents

Funny I should be writing this on a Saturday night. I'm wondering how many of my fellow ministry friends are spending Saturday nights quickly getting ready for the lessons we'll be teaching the next day? Maybe just me but I bet I'm not alone.

If you're reading this book, you're probably like me, an average Jill or Joe working or volunteering in a small church. Rick had solid stuff to say in this chapter, but here was what was running through my mind: "It sounds right on, Rick. But how do I translate all this to being a better teacher in my confirmation class? Sunday school class? Youth group? Small group Bible study?"

I can sum it up with one phrase: Make it R.E.A.L. With full credit to the folks at Group Publishing, it's the best way to make sure your students are getting the message on the inside—where it counts. Group believes in these teaching principles so much that they're in the very DNA of everything Group does. (Can you tell I'm their No. 1 fan?)

This is what I mean by making your teaching R.E.A.L.:

Relational
Whatever you do, fill your teaching time with relationship-building opportunities. More important than your students building a relationship with you, it's essential they build faith friendships with their peers. That's a skill they can take into their world. The quality of the way your students build relationships with others is often mirrored in the quality of their relationship with God.

So how do you make you teaching style more relational?

- Provide a safe environment where no one ridicules or blabs

- Use pair shares or small group discussion so everyone opens up

- Decrease your talking time and increase theirs

- Ask questions that start out low risk and then move into deeper sharing

- Give opportunities for students to continue supporting one another after class is over

- Go through learning experiences together to build relationships (mission trips, camping, feeding the poor, leading VBS, and so on)

Experiential

Think about a significant lesson you've learned in your life. Was it learned in a sermon? From TV? From a real-life event? All the best lessons I've learned are from something I did or shouldn't have done, an experience I lived out. That's also how most of your students are wired to learn—by experience. So bring those experiences into your circle of learning:

- Get your kids inside the Bible story. For example, for the Burning Bush story, sit around a fire pit and have your kids take off their shoes.

- Rather than talk about a Christ-like principle, help your kids experience the principle and THEN talk about it. Serving the poor is a much faster way to learn about compassion than just talking about it in a Bible study.

- Experiential learning involves everyone, not just the teacher or the extroverts in the class.

- Every experience is a teachable moment. Trust the Holy Spirit process.

Applicable

Having extolled the virtues of providing experiences for your students, let me say experiences are worthless if you miss the application step in a lesson time together. It's just wasted time if your students walk away knowing the biblical details of a story without making a life connection in their hearts. Life application is key.

This is why it's so important to debrief an activity or experience AFTER it happens, gleaming all the "aha" moments. Here are four key question categories to ask in making an experience really apply to the lives of your youth:

1. First, ask debriefing questions: "What happened? How did it feel when you...? What was going through your mind while you were...?"

2. Move next to interpretation questions: "How was this experience like or unlike (whatever Bible principle you want to guide your class toward)?"

3. Put Scripture reading here. "What does the Bible add to our experience?"

4. Finish with application questions: "Because of this experience, I will now..." "What did you discover from this experience and how will you apply it?"

Learner-based

Is your teaching or classroom style best for you or for your students? Some of you may be thinking the answer is that if it's best for you the teacher, then it IS best for the students. Not true. Our ultimate goal is to give our kids whatever it takes for them to learn what Jesus wants them to learn. To keep the lesson in their hearts for a lifetime. So are your habits in your comfort zone or theirs? Do you put your students' needs first?

Take the following teacher-based vs. learner-based personal inventory:

1. Are you communicating in ways your students communicate? (Text, e-mail, facebook, and so on.)

2. Is your teaching environment new and fresh with updated pictures, bulletin boards, paint, furniture, and free of distractions?

3. Do you do spend less than one-third of your class time talking?

4. Have you removed anything that looks even remotely like a pulpit, lectern, or podium from your classroom?

5. Are you set up to show DVD clips?

6. Do you have computer access available?

7. Are there teenager-friendly Bibles available for use?

8. Are you using a curriculum that includes all the R.E.A.L. principles?

9. Are you preparing your lesson well ahead of time and not on the run?

10. Are you getting to know your students beyond their names and grades?

If you answered "no" to one or two of the above questions, it's OK but make some tweaks. If you answered "no" to three or more, you need a serious teaching style overhaul. It can be done, but make sure to seek after God's heart in asking if you're serving in the right ministry.

Now these are the gifts Christ gave to the church: the apostles, the prophets, the evangelists, and the pastors and teachers. Their responsibility is to equip God's people to do his work and build up the church, the body of Christ. This will continue until we all come to such unity in our faith and knowledge of God's Son that we will be mature in the Lord, measuring up to the full and complete standard of Christ (Ephesians 4:11-13 NLT).

"Leadership is the catalyst for releasing God's 'what ifs' in others. Apparently God is totally fine with leadership coming in all shapes and sizes. The uniqueness we bring to the leadership task is what God uses to his advantage by placing us into snug-fit contexts. So we must make no mistake about it. Leadership is about God releasing his outlandish hopes and dreams through a certain time, with a certain people. That last phase is very important, for ultimately leadership is relational."[1]
—Ron Martoia)

What if everything we knew about leadership was completely backward and even unbiblical? What if we could've been doing it differently, even better, for centuries? What if we could develop teenagers and adults into leaders and not just followers?

You see, I think the church is long overdue for a leadership renovation. We've enjoyed reformation and restoration but not renovation. We desperately need a return to our original DNA. How "church" leadership structures operate in today's culture is more like 20th century American politics than first century divine order. We tend to lead more like Trump than Paul. In many smaller congregations, political machinery routinely derails godly plans and purposes.

Really? You don't say! In the local church? (Insert your own sarcasm here).

[1]Ron Martoia, *Morph! The Texture of Leadership for Tomorrow's Church* (Loveland, CO: Group Publishing, 2003): 38.

Furthermore, our processes for recruiting, retaining, and resourcing leaders tend to reproduce organizational dysfunctions and by default, our development of teenage leadership is equally stunted.

One of the great issues facing the contemporary church—and really our nation as a whole—is a dearth of leaders. That's why we need to rethink leadership development. Maybe we've missed something, and perhaps the smaller church is the perfect place to grow real leaders.

TAKE ME TO YOUR LEADER-LESS

In their insightful book on "leaderless organizations," Ori Brafman and Rod A. Beckstrom remind us of the difference between the starfish and the spider:

> With a spider, what you see is pretty much what you get. A body's a body, a head's a head, and leg's a leg. But starfish are very different. The starfish doesn't have a head. Its central body isn't even in charge. In fact, the major organs are replicated throughout each and every arm. If you cut the starfish in half, you'll be in for a surprise: the animal won't die, and pretty soon you'll have two starfish to deal with.[2]

Of course, the suggestion of "leaderless" is seriously unnerving and, even in Brafman and Beckstrom's view, slightly misleading. Leaders still exist but they operate much differently within a decentralized structure because leaders are working everywhere. The energy flows from the outside to the center, rather than from the axis to the edges.

[2]Ori Brafman and Rod A. Beckstrom, *The Starfish and the Spider: The Unstoppable Power of Leaderless Organizations* (New York: Penguin Books, 2006): 35.

Decentralization does not mean chaos, disorder, or inferiority. In fact, it's part of an organization's unique DNA.

Centralized government and control has dominated businesses, schools, politics, and churches for centuries, but particularly within the past 300 years. Modernity's affection for mechanization reproduced itself around hubs and spokes (like the airlines) and flow-chart structures where a central boss, dictator, lord, professor, or leader controlled vision and values. It even impacted city development, particularly noticeable within Mormon communities in the American West. When Mormons settled and built a community, the LDS Temple was ground zero. Every street and avenue rippled out from the center. Consequently, if you're in Salt Lake City and traveling 14th Street West you know you're exactly 14 blocks west of the temple. In many 18th and 19th century settlements, the church building was front and center. The steeple and bell called people to gather for worship, school, political rallies, entertainment, and emergencies. It's no wonder a facility became the face of religion.

Despite cultural mechanization, many pre-modern tribal cultures still operated without a central leader. The Apache Indians are spotlighted by Brafman and Beckstrom for their ability to adapt, change, evolve, and respond to crisis and conflict sans a central leader. In Apache culture, a spiritual guru and cultural guide named a Nant'an led the tribe. Geronimo was a classic Apache Nant'an. Apache culture was unique in that power laid within the individual, not a "chief." If Geronimo went to war, those who wanted to fight with him grabbed their guns, but it was socially acceptable to refuse, since "the phrase 'you should' doesn't even exist in the Apache language."[3]

[3]Ibid., 20.

"There is only one prediction about the future that I feel confident to make. During this period of random and unpredictable change, any organization that distances itself from its employees and refuses to cultivate meaningful relationships with them is destined to fail. Those organizations who will succeed are those that evoke our greatest human capacities—our need to be in good relationships, and our desire to contribute to something beyond ourselves. These qualities… are only available in organizations where people feel they are trusted and welcome, and where people know their work matters."

—Margaret J. Wheatley, management consultant and author
(Quoted by Ron A. Carucci in *Leadership Divided: What Emerging Leaders Need and What You Might Be Missing*)

Consequently, when the Spaniards came to destroy the Apache they couldn't kill the "starfish" tribe because every time they eliminated another Nant'an, several others emerged.

The Apache nation reflected a decentralized social structure that valued "flexibility, shared power, and ambiguity."[4] No one could predict their attacks, gauge their strength, or foil their plans. The Apaches had no central political machinery beyond these "chiefs" who were merely influential leaders with qualities like "industriousness, generosity, impartiality, forbearance, conscientiousness, and eloquence in language."[5] The Apaches only surrendered when Geronimo's band of 30-50 fighters and their families agreed to truce in the face of 5,000 U.S. troops![6]

To help understand the nature of "leaderless" organizations, Brafman and Beckstrom identified several major principles for decentralization:

- When attacked, a decentralized organization tends to become even more open and decentralized[7]

- It's easy to mistake starfish (decentralized organisms) for spiders (centralized organisms)

- An open system doesn't have central intelligence; the intelligence is spread throughout the system

- Open systems can easily mutate

- The decentralized organization sneaks up on you

Of course, if you've been paying attention, we've documented a number of cultural examples, mostly created by a web world, for decentralization, including Wikipedia, YouTube, and Facebook.

[4]Ibid., 21.
[5]http://en.wikipedia.org/wiki/Apache
[6]Ibid.
[7]*Brafman and Beckstrom*, Starfish and the Spider: *21–41*.

You could also add Skype and Craigslist to the list—along with Southwest Airlines' "point to point" flights (rather than the hub system). All of these organizations and entities are "leaderless" in nature and reflect an emerging new "starfish" paradigm that is sure to shift and possibly eradicate modern institutions.

And then there's the natural world, which has long worked through decentralized formats. Look at an anthill or beehive. The "queen" exists but the power is in the drones and workers. When a queen is captured, it's not the end, as several more colonies will sprout. This process is a mystery within nature. Queens have influence, but their demise doesn't destroy the colony—it actually distributes the colony. Or consider migrating geese. These beautiful migratory birds fly in a classic "V" pattern and routinely switch the point position to allow rest for longer flights. No single goose is more important. All work in tandem and lead when necessary. The power rests in all, not one.

THE LEADER-LESS BODY OF CHRIST

I also believe decentralized government was God's original design for his people. The Israelites gathered in tribes, and from the Exodus under Moses' leadership until their first political king named Saul, they operated beneath decentralized strategies, relying upon community-appointed prophets, judges, and priests. Joshua led them into battle and conquered Canaan but was never elevated to a king or political ruler. The tribes, which were large extended family groups, selected and ordained influential leaders—but again, no centralized emperor.

During the period of the judges, the Israelites enjoyed simultaneous and spontaneous emerging leaders, called by God, to provide deliverance from oppressive foreign rulers. But eventually, the Israelites bent to cultural influences.

In 1 Samuel 8, the Israelite elders approached Samuel and requested a king. They wanted Samuel to centralize their culture and politicize their nation.

This request greatly grieved Samuel and he reminded them of what kings do: demand slaves, assign more political rulers, and take their daughters, sons, servants, flocks, and herds. Despite this negative prognosis, the people still chose centralization and national Israel began the slow march toward moral and political failure and eventual captivity. It was clear God didn't want Israel to have a king. It was a theocracy not a democracy or aristocracy.

Centuries later, the church was launched from out of Roman (centralized) rule and Jewish (centralized) religion. It's not surprising to find God, yet again, operating from a decentralized design. The early church was "leaderless" for most of the first century. It had no denominational headquarters, no central staff or power base. In the beginning it located naturally within Jerusalem but when persecution drove the apostles from the city, the church spread virally through communities like Antioch, Philippi, Corinth, and Thessalonica. It wasn't until the fourth century when Constantine made Christianity a state religion and gave it political perks like church property and clergy salaries that Christianity settled in Rome (eventually becoming what we now know as the Roman Catholic Church). Centralization through bishops, cardinals, and popes organized the church around power centers. But was this God's original design or desire?

In the New Testament, the early church seems clearly decentralized by natural blueprint. A group of older spiritual leaders (elders) were appointed to guide and guard the community of faith. Another group of men and women (deacons/deaconesses) were ordained to lead various ministries. There was no paid staff. No central pastor. No executive minister. No power centers.

The apostles were like starfish arms, and while Peter and Paul get a lot of play, the influence of the remaining 10 cannot be missed. According to tradition, John pastored the Ephesian church with great influence upon Christianity, producing disciples like Polycarp, who mentored Irenaeus. Tradition says Bartholomew ventured far into Asia, Andrew to Greece, and Thomas to India, to name only a few. It's interesting that the Jerusalem church wasn't led by an apostle but by James, the brother of Jesus.

Leadership in the first century church was driven by the community. The power was in the hands not the head. After all, Jesus was the head of the church not a person (Ephesians 5:23). In fact, in 1 Corinthians 12, the church is described as a body where every part has purpose and responsibility. And while some parts receive more applause and adoration, that doesn't mean lesser parts are invalid or inferior. In high school I broke my left pinkie finger playing football. It impacted every part of my life, from writing (I'm a leftie) to typing to chores to driving. You don't realize how much you use your pinkie until it's nonfunctional.

I hear ya since I just broke my right thumb and I'm right-handed. I can't even pull my pants up without help. Was that TMI?

Our bodies are essentially decentralized. If they weren't you couldn't have organ transplants, amputations, and appendectomies.

It's possible to be brain-dead and still functionally alive. It's possible for your heart to cease beating and lungs to stop breathing and be dead, yet still have active brain waves. Why is that? We are decentralized systems. Yes, death will come when the major systems are shut down for too long, but that's true of any living organism or organization.

The smaller church operates best when it decentralizes leadership. Youth ministries in smaller churches develop new leaders far better when we return to decentralized values. *It's not me but we.* It's not about staff structure but organizational system. It's not about plans or policies but values and vision. The larger a church (or anything) becomes the greater temptation to centralize power. But by tethering control to a hub of influence we actually short-circuit the leadership development process. The early church was full of leaders because everyone had a role and a function. When persecution drove them underground these leaders exploded like Apaches on the against the Spaniards. But that doesn't mean there weren't individuals pressing for centralized power. In Revelation 2:6, Jesus shares his distaste for "Nicolaitans," which some Bible scholars believe were individuals who oppressed the people (hence the name: niko [victory] and laos [people]).

Church leadership, according to Frank Viola and George Barna in *Pagan Christianity?: Exploring the Roots of our Church Practices,* started to "formalize at about the time of the death of the itinerant apostolic workers."[8] This is an important point. If we don't continually reproduce our leadership DNA it can eventually mutate into something far from original design. That's what happened in the church toward the end of the first century.

[8]Frank Viola, *Pagan Christianity: Exploring the Roots of our Church Practices* (Carol Stream: Tyndale House Publishers, 2008): 110.

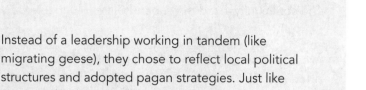

Instead of a leadership working in tandem (like migrating geese), they chose to reflect local political structures and adopted pagan strategies. Just like Roman rule, the second century church began to organize around a single leader of influence.

The primary voice to this leadership shift was Ignatius of Antioch (A.D. 35-107) who openly argued for a single-bishop rule. Ignatius believed a centralized absolute power was what the church needed and wrote:

> *"Plainly therefore we ought to regard the bishop as the Lord himself...It is not lawful apart from the bishop either to baptize or to hold a love feast, but whatever he shall approve, this is well-pleasing to God...Do nothing without the bishop...You should look on your bishop as a type of Father."[9]*

Two millennia later Ignatius' words still haunt how we lead in the church, particularly the smaller congregation. It's another reason I believe youth ministry can potentially release the death grip that single-rule centralization holds on the church and help congregations everywhere return to a biblical leadership vision. The leadership in many smaller churches tends to be centralized control usually through a pastor or a lead elder/deacon. Yet many smaller churches are already decentralized in leadership system. The smaller the church, the more likely the community has appointed a patriarch or matriarch to rule. This could be a founding figure or VIF (very important family). It's not until a congregation releases pastoral control to an outside person (incoming pastor) that the system centralizes. Outside leaders come with agendas, ideas, and personal preferences.

[9]Ibid., 111.

The community, if it desires, bends its will to the new guy.

Any of you have a VIF in your church? I like this reference, Rick. I have to put it out there that the appointment of such a family isn't intentional but emotional. It just happens and it's a good/evil thing. VIFs can be the people who get things done when needed. But VIFs can also be a roadblock to change by sheer numbers when something comes up for a vote. Life in the smaller church.

LEADERSHIP IN YOUTH MINISTRY

Small church youth pastors struggle with leadership issues all the time. It's either because the congregation has dumped the job in their lap and released control (since you're the one with the diploma and that's why we hired you) or it's a continual fight to wrest control from either the senior pastor or an influential lay leader. I remember how the church leaders cornered me once to explain their "vision" for youth ministry in that small church. One of the elders mentioned a "hootenanny" (I had no idea what that was) and a hayride to draw kids, and then shared several strategies I should do to attract area teenagers. I felt insulted. I was hired as their "youth expert," nearly owned a master's degree in religious education, and had over five years of church experience. And this old guy with bad hair is telling me how to program?

You see I had misunderstood the issue. Leadership is influence. I was influencing the teenagers in my ministry but failed miserably to impact the leaders. *Leaders don't produce followers; they reproduce leaders.*

And the inherent problem with centralized power—whether in a pastor, volunteer staff, or a group of teenagers—is that success is defined by how many are following you. It's the Twitter age, right? It doesn't matter if you're changing anything or developing leaders as much as do you have a "following." (Translation: How many attended? How big is your staff?)

Consequently, it's very easy to create a top-down leadership model, with you standing as a solitary general at the summit. All the vision, ideas, programming, and resources flow from you. Your ministry looks like the spider. Sure, you may lose a leg (volunteer) now and then, but if you recruit well you'll replace it. What happens when you lose several legs (volunteers) and the ones you recruit are hardly able to stand, let alone walk? In a centralized power system we usually respond one of two ways: guilt or gimmicks. We recruit by shame. *"If you don't do it, who will?" "I really need you, and if you don't join our team I don't know what I'll do." "The kids love you and need you. Do it for them!"*

Unfortunately guilt motivates only those gullible enough not to say "no." Consequently we lower our recruiting standards, especially in the smaller church, to enthusiastically embrace any warm body. We also relax training guidelines and policies to retain workers. *"I'd like you to show up 15 minutes early, but if you can't make that commitment I understand. We need you." "I should do a background check on you, but since I know you pretty well I'll look the other way."* Sound familiar? It happens all the time.

Of course, when guilt fails some of us move to desperation gimmicks. These can be tricky, but that's the point. *"Be a volunteer for the Crowder concert and I'll give you a free ticket to the event." "I really need a female volunteer for this overnight trip.*

If you do it I've got a $30 gift certificate to Applebee's in your name. Who wants it?" Sometimes the guilt and gimmicks work. They attract that "magical" volunteer that's been lurking in the shadows, but most of the time what we lure are volunteers better avoided. There are three types of people in a church: winners, whiners, and 'weeners. About 15 percent are winners (and you only need one on your team), while 15 percent are whiners (avoid these types at all costs). The remaining 70 percent are 'weeners or "betweeners" who will follow the power sources—either positive (winners) or negative (whiners). Depending on which way you lean, your congregation will either attract more enthusiastic champions or become a haven for dissatisfied grumblers.

In decentralized "leaderless" organizations the power and influence continually flows from the edges, which is why you must have winners providing the energy. Your responsibility is empowerment. You inspire greatness, instill integrity, and influence change by releasing the power to your volunteers and teenagers. This is perfectly and naturally suited for smaller church scenarios, many of which will never employ a professional youth minister. Imagine the energy and enthusiasm a youth ministry would spread if everyone owned the work. Imagine the workload being distributed by talent and passion and purpose. Imagine gatherings, calendars, events, and other activities created by the community. It's easier than you think. The problem is those who attempt to shift to such a philosophy still try to do it through centralized control. *I've decided that I want everyone to do something. I've created this new leadership approach where we all have a part.* Do you sense the centralization in those statements? It's about "I" not "us." It's about "me" not "we."

Decentralization happens when we completely abandon our own need for leadership control—and if you're reading this book I'm assuming you're the leader wanting the answers! What would happen if you stepped down? Walked away? Resigned? Would your youth ministry stumble and stall, even stop? That's the problem with "spiders"—kill the head and the whole thing dies. But you can't destroy a starfish with amputation alone. You can't kill a colony of ants or a hive of bees just by razing their homes. You can't stop geese from migrating if you shoot the lead goose. And you won't stop the church that's recaptured a decentralized leadership DNA.

THE STARFISH SMALLER CHURCH

So what's a starfish leadership look like? Brafman and Beckstrom outline five "legs" of decentralized organizations, each with specific applications to smaller church youth ministry.[10] These "legs" operate naturally in both developing teenagers into leaders and volunteers into ministry. The goal is to create a community of youth leaders—young and old—that rely on one another's talents, strength, creativity, and enthusiasm. It's a win-win.

Leg One: Circles

A core feature of decentralization is the circle not the square. Squares have corners that box, protect, hide, and define. You can't hide in a circle. There's no way to be cornered. You're either in or you're out. Decentralized circles are everywhere in cyber culture. Look at someone else's Facebook page and see a circle of "mutual friends." Join a fantasy football league—public or private—and you've joined a circle.

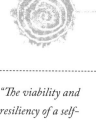

"The viability and resiliency of a self-organizing system comes from its great capacity to adapt as needed, to create structures that fit the moment. Neither form nor function alone dictates how the system is organized. Instead, they are process structures, reorganizing into different forms in order to maintain their identity."

—Margaret J. Wheatley, management consultant and author *Leadership and the New Science: Discovering Order in a Chaotic World*

[10]Brafman and Beckstrom, Starfish and the Spider: 88-101.

You don't even have to play, and in fantasy sports nearly a third of every league features non-participating managers. People join and play if they want.

In youth ministry this has tremendous implications for how we grow leaders. Conventional wisdom argued a person needed to meet certain qualifications, membership requirements, or job description. Create the box and form-fit everyone else to it. But circles are fluid and flow freely. They're rooted in autonomy and independence.

Start by looking at your youth leadership team as the entire congregation. Every person is on the team. Now start drawing a circle. Let's say someone has offered their swimming pool to you for a party on a particular date.

You announce the date (draw a circle) and invite others to make the party fly.

So someone else offers to barbeque burgers. Another person has a guitar and thinks it would be fun to lead some worship. Another elderly gentleman hands you $100 to buy any supplies while a stay-at-home "creative" mom volunteers to promote the event. Teenagers also get involved. One starts a "No School Pool Party" fan page at Facebook. Another virally begins a text message campaign. Still another kid hears about the guy with the guitar and wants to accompany (you say OK!). The party grows from the ground up. Everybody is asked to bring a little something to eat.

And what's your role? Resources and reminders. You keep everyone in the loop, but if someone decides not to follow through or outside forces create the need for new plans, something else takes its place. Rain just forces the party indoors. The burger chef bails, but there are still chips and desserts.

Even if the pool is suddenly inoperable it's just an easy switch to a local city park and pool.

In a circle, everyone is in and equal. Your responsibility might be different or greater, but no single person steers the ship. This creates a natural problem about control. No rules suggest anarchy and chaos. However, as Outback Steakhouse proclaims: *No rules can be just right*. In a circle, it's about norms not laws. As Brafman and Beckstrom note, "The norms, in fact, become the backbone of the circle. Because they realize that if they don't enforce the norms no one will, members enforce the norms with one another."[11] This creates mutual accountability and, in fact, can be more effective than top-down enforcement. The rules spread as part of the community culture, not the leader's whims, desires, or ideas.

Circles are naturally rich in community. Trust emerges as those within the ring invest time and treasure.

Resources are shared. Relationships are deepened. Sadly, many volunteer teams are fragmented and innately selfish out of mistrust or fear of failure, rejection, or reprisal. Decentralized strategies restore community and unleash contribution. This is the biblical pattern of Paul's church planting strategy. He started churches across Asia Minor simply by creating circles of community. He'd start by building relationships at a local synagogue or community square, then he eventually expanded into homes.

Leg Two: The Catalyst
In chemistry, nitrogen and hydrogen are common elements that easily co-exist without any change. But something happens when you add iron to nitrogen and hydrogen: It creates the explosive element ammonia.

[11]Ibid., 90.

The irony (pun intended) is that ammonia contains no iron! For some mysterious reason, iron causes nitrogen and hydrogen to fuse and then disappears. Chemists refer to iron as a "catalyst" or "any element or compound that initiates a reaction without fusing into that reaction."[12]

In decentralized organizations, control is ceded to the community, but that doesn't mean there are no influencers. Catalysts are change-agents. Like iron with hydrogen and nitrogen, they create combustion and forge new elements. And yet, when you study the situation, these catalysts are nowhere to be found. Catalysts initiate change and then step out of the way. They guide and guard—but from side stage. Like the proverbial stage manager they live in the wings but keep the script moving and the actors on spot.

What's truly remarkable is that a catalyst can be anyone.

The starfish only moves when one of its legs persuades the others to join the cause. It's about communal cooperation. No single person controls the vision, but everyone cooperates around a common voice. As Brafman and Beckstrom relate, "In letting go of the leadership role, the catalyst transfers ownership and responsibility to the circle."[13] The catalyst can't be a one-person show or some power-hungry dictator. The catalyst enlists, energizes, endorses, educates, and then exits. A cultural example of a catalyst is Osama bin Laden. His al-Qaida terror network is inspired and influenced by his leadership but thrives upon far lesser commanders. Even if he were captured or killed (which at the time of this writing had not happened), it wouldn't end al-Qaida. Another catalyst would emerge.

A more positive and better example of catalyst leadership is Jesus Christ.

[12]Ibid., 92.
[13]Ibid., 93.

If anybody could've set up a centralized political powerhouse it was Jesus. He could've ruled with an iron fist but chose rather to influence (like iron) and develop followers into leaders. He particularly translated his vision into 12 men who were hardly notable or newsworthy. Jesus revealed you could change the world with ordinary Joes and Janes. You don't need political pundits, media personalities, or American Idols. And Jesus didn't wait long to release his disciples into ministry. Nearly immediately he began to transfer ownership to his disciples. They were barely prepared before Christ sent them on their first mission (Mark 6:6b-13). But unlike power-driven cult personalities, Jesus wasn't planning to stick around. He wasn't building a royal dynasty but a divine kingdom.

It's easy in youth ministry to hunger to build legacies. It's only natural to leave a mark. However, catalysts mark their community, and then leave. The best test of decentralized leadership is a resignation. Too many smaller churches are trapped by cults of personality. It's not about the community but the point person. *"If we just had a hip youth minister, we'd be fine." "We need someone who can lead worship that kids today like." "Stay away from anyone over 30. We want a young pastor."*

Catalyst youth workers continually create new circles and move on—even in the same congregation. They inspire change and fuse new directions, and then step away. It's about reproduction and reinvention. We need to continually equip adolescents to assume leadership roles and resource volunteers to effective service.

Leg Three: Ideology
Any catalyst can create a circle and form a community but the tie that binds is a common vision.

Online communities like eBay, fantasy sports, Craigslist, and Facebook carve circles of accepted and desirable connection points. These connections translate into ideologies. We belong because we believe. We participate in an online auction or league because it's good friendly fun. Through Facebook many people have rediscovered long-lost friends, but it's also a place for families to share memories and businesses, schools, and churches to champion a cause. Our experiences create connections—friendships—around an engaging idea. Our belief in that scheme creates affection and adoration, love and loyalty. We participate because it's changed our lives for the better. We sacrifice because other suitors might tempt, but they can never satisfy.

The key to recruiting talent is a vibrant community focused upon a singular life-changing cause. It's hard to find a job at Southwest Airlines these days. People retire, but they don't quit. Maybe because the Southwest way is deeply rooted in an engaging ideology:[14]

- Dare to be disciplined, reap the rewards

- Hire for attitude, train for skills

- Think small, act fast

- Ask questions, think results

- Stay fresh, stretch to grow

- Be creative, color outside the lines

- Create a legendary culture

- Preserve what you value

- Revel in your accomplishments

[14]This list is the outline of chapters from the bestselling book on Southwest Airlines: *Nuts! Southwest Airlines' Crazy Recipe for Business and Personal Success* by Kevin and Jackie Freiberg (New York: Broadway Books, 1997).

- Honor those you love

- Make work fun

- Give back—it's the right thing to do

- Great service begins at home

What's the ideology for your youth ministry? How many of the above statements could translate to your situation? Decentralized leadership empowers the team around common goals, values, and vision. Do you manufacture a disciplined culture that encourages volunteers to grow in skill and understanding? Do you recruit people with great attitudes or simply those who finally give in? Do you spawn innovation and spark creativity? Do you celebrate success and honor achievement? Is your youth ministry a fun place (for teenagers and volunteers)? Do you serve others regularly? Do you meet the needs of your own crowd first?

Ideology is what cements loyalty and deepens commitment. People won't quit on something they believe in nor will they leave what makes them feel whole, real, and connected.

Leg Four: The Preexisting Network

In 2009 a political phenomenon emerged across America known as "tea parties." These grassroots, loosely organized, conservative gatherings started on April 15 to protest big government, taxes, universal health care proposals, and a host of other agendas. These rallies, promoted on conservative talk radio, mushroomed to include countless communities. On September 12, 2009, a major gathering in Washington, D.C., drew tens of thousands of "tea party" protesters, including many fringe groups from across the political spectrum.

"The organization of a living system bears no resemblance to organizational charts. Life uses networks; we still rely on boxes. But even as we draw our boxes, people are ignoring them and organizing as life does, through networks of relationships. To become effective at change, we must leave behind the imaginary organization we design and learn to work the real organization, which will always be a dense network of interdependent relationships."

—Margaret J. Wheatley, management consultant and author *Leadership and the New Science: Discovering Order in a Chaotic World*

The tea parties are a perfect example of a leaderless organization and decentralized structure, and they reveal how such systems rely upon preexisting networks to procreate and propagate. The tea parties leaned upon conservative talk show "catalysts" to emblazon courage and embolden commitment, but it was local community networks already in place where the power truly originated.

In essence, decentralization doesn't mean you reinvent the wheel. Rather you flex muscle and marketing from individuals already within the system. The Internet and cell phone create instant connection and rapid responses to virally promote a message.

But how does this all work in volunteer and leadership development? First of all, the best recruiter isn't you but your team. Your teenagers are the best (and worst) advertisement for meetings and events. Your volunteers' satisfaction and enjoyment of their work is the best recruiting tool.

Secondly, you have untapped preexisting networks all around you in the smaller church like senior citizens, worship teams, parents, empty nesters, and college students, to name a few. Too often we tap a particular group so much we drain it dry. Some of my best youth workers were over 65, a mom or dad, a lonely divorcee, or an energetic collegian. Finally, the power of the network is in marketing. Use it. You don't need every senior saint to volunteer but why can't they all become your "fans?"

I'll be honest—I've found recruiting to be a simple process once I got out of the way. Empower your team and create a leadership culture so attractive nobody wants to quit and you'll discover volunteers lining up to participate.

Leg Five: The Champion

The two most important people in early church history were Peter and Paul. Peter's influence among the Jews and Paul's impact with the Gentiles created a perfect one-two punch for spreading the gospel across the Roman empire. Jesus was the catalyst, but Peter and Paul became the champions.

Every cause needs a champion. These individuals differ from catalysts in that they are fiercely committed to the cause. Catalysts have charisma, but champions have conviction. They're next-level leaders who take the original vision and move it beyond imagination. That's what happened at Southwest Airlines in 2001. While other airlines were decimated by the September terrorist attacks, Southwest continued to be profitable despite the semi-retirement of its charismatic founder Herb Kelleher. Stepping into Kelleher's shoes were Jim Parker as CEO and Colleen Barrett as president. Three years later Parker retired and Gary Kelly assumed control.

And in 2008, Kelly also took over Barrett's role after she stepped down from her position. That's what makes Southwest Airlines remarkable. Unlike other airlines that continually replace, retire, or fire CEOs, Southwest just reloads another "champion" because the company is loaded with champs. Of course, since the lion's share of the decisions originates within lower-level supervisors, ramp personnel, and gate agents, there are plenty of people to appoint and anoint.

In the smaller church, there are undoubtedly numerous youth ministry "champions" in the wings. And in decentralized systems, these champions rise with the task, advocate the cause, and inspire the team to success.

Like catalysts, when they're gone, another champion emerges. In the first century church, Paul and Peter's deaths didn't destroy the emerging young faith but only made it explode.

If you're wondering where all your "champs" are hanging out, you're probably stuck in a centralized hierarchy. Champions emerge when catalysts call. The problem for many smaller church youth workers is that we prefer to steer the ship. True catalysts inspire champions to take the helm and don't mind failure (Peter sinking in water, denials) or flaw (Paul's perfectionism, impatience).

Smaller churches and their youth ministries are perfect opportunities to shift to leader-less decentralized structures. The natural rhythms and seasons of a smaller setting make it easier to thinking small and fast. The size of a smaller congregation creates opportunity to be communal and develop leadership in both teenagers and adults for works of ministry.

There are few things that matter more than translating and transferring the DNA of your church to the next generation.

The future of your congregation is tied to catalysts and champions. These individuals might be 13 or 30 so don't let age limit your vision. If you are the catalyst, work yourself out of a job. If you are a champion, keep duking it out.

Leaders aren't born. Leaders are cultivated. They fly in formation waiting for their chance to assume point. They buzz and busy themselves within ordinary tasks until crisis creates opportunity. Leaders emerge from the wings, the shadows, and the bottoms. They may not look like much, but it's about attitude not aptitude. Leaders are everywhere.

That's why it's slightly misleading to call decentralized organizations "leader-less." It suggests nobody is leading when, in reality, everyone is to one degree or another.

In a 21C culture, the paradigm has shifted. Conventional top-down boss management strategies will fail to attract and endear emerging generations. Centralized systems are failing, including in the church, and the smaller congregation possesses decided advantages to slam it in reverse and return to a biblical decentralized leadership culture.

It's time to migrate. It's time to fly.

Steph's 2Cents

"Your responsibility is empowerment. You inspire greatness, instill integrity, and influence change by releasing the power to your volunteers and teenagers. This is perfectly and naturally suited for smaller church scenarios, many of which will never employ a professional youth minister. Imagine the energy and enthusiasm a youth ministry would spread if everyone owned the work." — Rick Chromey

What can I add? Rick has given us a really good chapter here on leadership in youth ministry within the smaller church. From my viewpoint, he's spot-on about the need to be decentralized—but come on! The truth is that as we read this, we know if we're going to be REALLY "leaderless" we'd have to start all over. Tear apart a few square, in-the-box leadership structures to allow new interlocking circles to float into place.

So let's dream what a new leadership structure would (could) look like. Don't worry; I won't make you show it to anyone.

Just doodling here; no one has to see who and what we're including. More importantly, who and what we're NOT including.

Your Ministry's Five Legs of Leadership

The Circles

Do what Rick says and take a look at your whole congregation. Consider them all a part of the youth circle of influence. Take the time to gather info and have a ready chart to look at who's in your youth circle.

Who does what for a living? (For example: We have two pro football players who attend our church and have been generous with free tickets.)

What talents or abilities are available?

_____

_____

Who has what connection to what people, places, and things? _____

_____

Who has access to interesting spaces? _____

_____

What vehicles do people own? _____

_____

Who can be tapped for:

Food _____

Money _____

Games _____

Tickets _____

Creativity _____

Decorating_____

Carpentry _____

Sports _____

Pool _____

Big-screen TV _____

Lake/retreat house _____

Sewing _____

Artistry _____

Computer skills _____

Writers _____

Drama _____

Music _____

Other _____

The Catalysts

Identify the catalysts for change within your church. In my humble opinion, these people can produce positive and/ or negative change. Knowing who they are and how they affect the youth ministry is just plain ol' wise on your part.

1. _____

2. _____

3. _____

4. _____

5. _____

If you listed any negative-effect catalysts, what can/should you do about their influence?

The Ideology

We're not talking about your youth ministry vision or goals here. Your group's ideology may be hard to pinpoint, yet I'm sure it's alive and active within the working of your ministry. Think of your group's belief system, those rules for living that exist with your group's ministry.

Some are spoken and some are subtle. But they're there and they guide what your group REALLY says, does, and believes. Try to put your group's beliefs into one paragraph:

_____

_____

_____

_____

_____

Was this hard to do? Are you sure that what you wrote for your group's belief system is what your kids would write? Suggestion: Take this activity home and ask your kids to write down the beliefs of the group. You may be pleasantly surprised. Or not so much.

The PreExisting Networks

I don't find it hard to recruit either, Rick. But you and I have been around the recruiting block a few times, haven't we?

What's my secret? Let your people recruit their own people. If you have all these little circles of leadership (starfish) working within your youth ministry, why would it make ANY sense for you to figure out who does what within them? It makes WAY more sense for you to let each "starfish" find its own legs. For example: I hate to cook and all things "kitchen" except that which is produced in it. So when I ask someone to take on putting together a meal for the group, I stay out of it from there.

What preexisting teams do you have? Which ones do you need to back out of and hand over ownership?

The Champions

Who are your ministry's champions? List them right here:

_____

_____

_____

_____

_____

It's true: Good leadership really is working yourself out of a job. My ministry's champions? Scott, Tara, Heather, Carol, Sean, Steve, Jordan, Ty, Tracey, and Wayne. These are the folks who took on a piece of our ministry and are running with it! They are the true champions of what they do in our ministry. They've become the experts, and I bow to their knowledge. I don't have to control everything.

I just get them coffee.

CHAPTER ELEVEN ◎ DYNO-MITES!

> *Then a poor widow came by and dropped in two small coins. "I tell you the truth," Jesus said, "this poor widow has given more than all the rest of them. For they have given a tiny part of their surplus, but she, poor as she is, has given everything she has" (Luke 21:2-4 NLT).*
>
> *You want what you don't have, so you scheme and kill to get it. You are jealous of what others have, but you can't get it, so you fight and wage war to take it away from them. Yet you don't have what you want because you don't ask God for it (James 4:2 NLT).*

The recession of 2009 had everyone living lean.

I hope that by the time you read this chapter, the American economy will be hunky dory or at least back to whatever we call "normal" these days. But if not, and the money is still tight, let's all take a deep breath and remember when cash flowed more freely and forcefully.

In the mid-1990s and into the beginning of the new century, our economy was in overdrive. The Dow Jones Industrial Average jetted well above 10,000. Housing prices were in the stratosphere. Our vehicles were high-end Hummers and Harleys. Everybody was up to their neck in debt but didn't seem to mind.

The September 2001 terrorist attacks cracked the bubble that finally and fully burst in late 2007.

Suddenly the American economy went into free fall. Stocks nose-dived, and 401Ks became 201Ks. Banks shut down. Auto companies went bankrupt. Home mortgages ballooned and forced countless foreclosures. Gas prices shot to over $4 a gallon. Major airlines folded, as did seemingly secure tech businesses like Circuit City and CompUSA.

In 2008 and 2009 we entered into a full-blown recession. Millions joined the unemployment lines and pushed the national jobless rate past 10 percent—with many states nursing a 15 percent rate.

When the jobs folded, so did wallets. Consumers grew edgy and stopped frivolous and excessive spending. Restaurants struggled as diners opted for home meals. Small businesses stalled and many failed. Gas prices fell as supply grew greater than demand. Even major holidays like Halloween and Christmas couldn't shake the economic doldrums. The stock market stabilized but seemed stagnant, unable to push too high before investors sold off and tumbled profits once again. Despite government stimulus, cash-for-clunker auto deals, and bailouts, no amount of money infused into the national economy could jump start it. Even the global economy was flat.

Churches were not immune to the recession.

In fact, one of the unknown stories was the number of churches—especially in sunshine states like Florida, Arizona, and California—that were teetering on foreclosure notices. Many congregations enjoyed growth during this same economic boon, including some that climbed into megachurch status, so facilities and staff were added without much consideration. One church I know proudly announced it wanted to be as "deep in debt as possible when Jesus returned." Today that congregation is shedding staff and programs to pay the bills. I wonder what Jesus thinks about its financial plan?

Naturally, smaller churches have also seen a dip in the offering dollars, but unlike larger congregations, they have managed to survive through leaner budgets and spending freezes.

Since staff and facility bills are minimal, especially in established small churches, the recession pinched but it did not punch out programs and ministries.

The primary problem that fueled the recession was greed. The American dream for a bigger home, boat, car, or lifestyle got the best of many people. You can't live high on the hog if you're making peanuts, but a lot of people did, using easy credit and jumbo loans to finance their stuff. When the mortgages ballooned, gas prices spiked, the pink slip delivered, and the savings dwindled, the wake-up call phoned in.

BUILDING EMPIRES...

American families weren't the only greedy ones. The church followed a similar path of "church envy" and erected monster stadium-style buildings with exorbitant lighting, sound, and video systems. New vans, buses, computer systems, and other pricey high-tech toys were purchased. Staff salaries rose to record highs. I knew several youth pastors in Southern California that were pulling six-figure incomes. Granted, it was California but still—six figures?!?

Six figures, huh? Just where were those churches? Hey, I make six figures depending on your viewpoint on the decimal.

The smaller church wasn't blameless either. Many congregations upgraded their sound/computer systems and purchased high-end video projectors in order to add PowerPoint slides to sermons and songs. Many smaller congregations emptied their coffers to hire their first professional youth ministers.

As a youth ministry professor I routinely fielded calls from small church preachers, elders, and deacons wondering if I had any "good" students to recommend for hire. In my conversation, I'd always ask for a description of their church, and nearly every time I heard their current attendance plus the enigmatic tag *"but we're growing."* *"We're running 125 but we're growing."* *"Last Sunday we had 90 but we're growing."* The solution to "grow" more was to spend more money on a "professional" youth minister—even if he was a kid still wet with Bible 101 and Intro to Youth Work classes behind his ears.

In a sense this professionalization of the youth pastorate, especially in the smaller church, created an ecclesiastical Frankenstein. Mid-sized churches couldn't keep youth pastors (pay was low) when larger congregations came knocking with bigger salaries, gyms, youth staffs, and cushy budgets. As megachurches swiped staff from medium-sized churches, these congregations returned the favor by hunting hires from the smaller churches. The smaller congregations had nowhere to turn but their local ministry schools, Bible colleges, and Christian universities to snag a youth minister. Of course, hiring inexperienced and mildly educated "pros" has its drawbacks. Consequently, many small church youth ministries suffered from constant turnover and few realized any real "growth" from their decision to go "pro." In fact, smaller congregations soon discovered by the turn of the 21st century that ministry graduates— especially the best and brightest—were now being hired by medium and large churches, leaving a low talent pool for the undersized.

This phenom has been true for my own youth ministry career. Over my 30 years, I made more than a couple (but less than several) moves out of a smaller church (and salary) into a bigger church ministry.

I'd like to say the decision was based solely on hearing God's call, but let's just say God often used the fact that I could better "provide" for my family in the move. True also for small churches finding themselves unable to sustain a consistent youth worker thus unable to build a sustainable youth ministry. I do consultant work for a well-known youth ministry assessment firm out of Nashville, Tennessee, and we see this dynamic repeatedly in assessing smaller churches. Why? Youth workers have to eat, too.

That's why I always smiled when another church of a 100 called for a youth minister. In 15 years as youth ministry professor and matchmaker for churches and my students, I saw the part-time salary skyrocket. In the late 1980s, a weekend youth minister might get $100 for two days of ministry, but by 2000 some churches were paying up to $250 weekly for a top-end student plus benefits like tuition, paid holidays, and book and conference allowances. One of my graduating students was even wooed by two different smaller congregations with a "signing bonus!"

All's fair in love, war, and youth ministry.

GENERATIONAL BOOM

Another piece to the church financial puzzle was a generational leadership transition in the mid-1980s as "thirtysomething" boomers assumed control of aging "Depression-era" elder boards, groups, and leadership teams. In the smaller church the tipping point of control came slightly later, but when it did everything changed. In my early youth ministries I served under mostly "Depression-era" leaders who were marked by hard financial times. A penny earned was a penny saved. Spend what you make. Don't sell the farm.

These frugal leaders sheltered tens of thousands of dollars for the rainy day. I worked as a summer youth intern for a western Kansas church of 250 where church coffers were as full as the wheat silos. A great harvest meant fantastic offerings. A lean yield caused giving to drop accordingly.

The boomer generation's ascent of America's boardroom in the 1980s also reached the church house. The boomers' mentality was vastly different from their elders. *You spent money to make money. Debt was fine, especially debt that brought return. A penny earned was a nickel spent—in hopes a dime was on the way. Go ahead and sell the farm because, to quote generational mop top heroes, tomorrow never knows.* Consequently, church savings were opened and funds drained for stuff like computers, projectors, padded pews, and wireless microphones (not to mention family life centers, youth buildings, and additional staff). As many congregations, including a fair number of small churches, spent more money on facilities, curriculum, program resources, and salaries, they did see success and growth. The boomer generation was coming back to church in the 1980s and 1990s and found full bands, multimedia, and specialized staff an attractive amenity.

Consequently, many congregations enjoyed incredible growth, particularly "non-denominational" entities with young founding pastors (like Bill Hybels or Rick Warren) and brief histories. But not every church grew. In fact, most did not, especially churches of great congregational maturity or aging pastors. Mainline denominations were also hit hard as "community" churches became a drawing card for boomer families tired of ecclesiastical politics. It didn't matter how much money was infused into the church structure; nothing seemed to help.

It was like spending thousands for facelifts on a 90-year-old. Cosmetically, there was progress, but it didn't halt the death process.

WHERE YOUR HEART IS...

There's a good reason Jesus spoke so much about money. He understood the temptation to satisfy deep divine longings by stuffing them with stuff. He recognized the power of the dollar to impact priorities. Affluence has influence. *Where your treasure is, there your heart dwells. You can't serve both God and money. Sell your possessions and give it to the poor.*

One of my favorite biblical stories involves a widow living on her last dime. She comes to the temple one day to present her offering. In Jesus' day, this type of activity had some fanfare attached. The rich, in particular, loved to flaunt their wealth when dropping their required 10 percent in the kettles. Since coins were the currency of the day this caused no small racket. The more money a person gave the bigger the noise it created. You can imagine the scene in the temple. The sound of coins hitting the kettles created a continual clatter. Occasionally a large dollar dump would sound a high decibel and even momentarily halt the activity—which only brought additional favor and notoriety to the giver. It's in this noisy clamor that a widow quietly approaches a kettle and deposits her 2 cents worth. To the human ear, it was insignificant chump change, but to Jesus it was a divine sacrifice of epic proportions.

The widow didn't give 10 percent (as required by law) but 100 percent. She gave her last nickel. She had nothing else to offer and lived completely on faith that God would provide. In those days, you didn't have credit.

You survived on what you scrounged, and the poor, old, and disabled sought alms everywhere they could. We don't know where this widow got her two "mites." Maybe some rich man tossed her a couple pennies as a joke. All we know is she gave all and Jesus took notice.

In the movie *Jerry Maguire*, the classic line is "Show me the money!" We're also told to follow the money, and that's exactly what Jesus did. No one would've heard two tiny copper coins fall into a kettle except for God. In a noisy world where money talks pretty loud, who's going to notice a paltry two-bit sacrifice? And yet the widow's offering made more noise than all the rest. Sometimes you just have to have ears to see.

Let's be brutally honest. Smaller churches aren't going to enjoy massive amounts of financial capital, unless blessed with a significant estate from an affluent member. Many struggle to pay the utilities, mortgage, and pastor salary, let alone find extra funds for curriculum, equipment, and other programming needs. And when recession takes a bite out of everyone's wallet, it only exasperates the problem.

THE PURSUIT OF CHURCH HEALTH

Of course, few congregations truly consider how much of their spending is rooted in "keeping up with the Jones' First Church" down the street. We want to be like them, so we buy what they have—only to realize it doesn't produce the same results. A PowerPoint upgrade means nothing if no one uses it or operates it with excellence. To quote a political candidate, it's like putting lipstick on a pig. And why spend thousands of dollars on a weekend youth minister to babysit your teenagers?

It's great experience for the student pastor, but when he graduates or jumps to a larger church because you can't pay more (as he now has college loans to repay), what have you really gained?

The average church attracts $10 a week per person in giving. Simply put, if you have a 100-member church, you're probably garnering a grand in the plate or $52,000 annually. If you want to pay your preacher a living wage, half of that will go just to his salary. Another 10 percent is perhaps given to missions. That leaves 40 cents on the dollar to pay utilities, maintenance, insurance, and other necessities. The only way to spend more is to invest from whatever savings exists or deepen congregational debt. The former is a great option for situations with positive returns (like a computer, video projector, software, sound equipment, or website development) but if there's no gain or even negative consequence, it hurts the future. That's why I question a congregation that spends $100 a week to pay for inexperience (part-time youth minister) when it could better spend that $5,200 a year investing in its youth ministry volunteers.

I have to give you an "Amen" on that, Rick!

You could send your lay leaders to a high-powered youth ministry leadership conference and cover all expenses and still have money left over. You could subscribe every volunteer to Group Magazine to constantly feed them ideas and insights. You could invest in leadership retreats, curriculum, and programming materials.

It's interesting to note that some experts in church growth argue that when giving reaches $15 a week per person, it's the sign of a healthy congregation (remember, most give around $10 weekly).

Furthermore there's plenty of anecdotal evidence to suggest a congregation can adequately support one pastor for every 150 active members.

Both of these standards are wonderful barometers to identify when to add staff from a position of health, not wealth. The secret to church growth is really congregational *health*. Just like the human body, a congregation cannot grow unless its systems are functional and strong. When a child has leukemia or cystic fibrosis or heart murmurs, this condition will impact not only physical development but also lifespan prospects.

A church is no different.

That's partly why I saved the "money" chapter for last. You don't need more money. In fact, money might be your trouble. I spent some time as a financial life counselor and learned a lot about how money works. In fact, when your money works for you (rather than you for your money), you are financially solvent and successful. Too many congregations, especially smaller churches, work for their money. They haven't learned how to invest for future returns, network with other churches, or save for seasons of economic drought.

A lot of smaller church youth workers are constantly prowling for dollars. Many smaller churches use fundraisers to finance their programs and routinely milk their neighborhood and community as the cash cow. I used to do fundraisers all the time. In fact, I was pretty good at generating cash through pity or party, but I eventually grew weary and wary of my tactics. I finally saw the light during a bake sale at a local grocery store. We actually did well in the final dollar count, but I noticed the majority of sales were from youth ministry families (many of whom supplied the baked goods in the first place).

"When money is seen as a solution for every problem, money itself becomes the problem."

—Richard Needham

In other words, my kids' moms were slaving in the kitchen and buying back what they donated! I also realized the message I was sending both to my students and the neighborhood. We were no different than the guy on the corner with a sign that said "Out of work. Buy my cookies so I can feed my family." We were communicating to our neighbors their money was more important than their presence. Plus we weren't providing a service but only selling a product. I also noted my teenagers showed moments of embarrassment, especially when non-churched friends wandered by.

I decided to give up fundraising all together.

I hate fundraisers! (Unless they also provide a fellowship opportunity for the church like a dinner, program, and so on.) Don't even get me started on car washes! Why fundraisers begin with the word "fun" I'll never know!

BECOMING A FRIEND RAISER...

In fact, to quote a college president, I became a "friend raiser" instead. I developed relationships with significant individuals in our congregation, persons of affluence and influence. I discovered dozens of amazing resources—some even financial—that existed within my own congregation. One man owned a local White Castle restaurant. I asked him if he'd provide burgers and fries for a special youth event, and to my delight, he agreed (and threw in soda to boot!). Another family owned a beautiful pool and backyard play land. They agreed to let us host youth worker meetings and parties. I built friendships with senior saints, and more than one willingly gave cash to help needy students go on trips.

If networking works so well, why don't smaller churches do it? A primary reason is "fear."

- *Fear that kids will "church hop." It's a real fear, especially in congregations that aren't meeting teenagers' needs.*

- *Fear of losing control. What if kids don't study what we want them to study? Or sing songs we don't approve? Control is often a sign of leadership insecurity.*

- *Fear that beliefs will be compromised. This is an honest fear and only problematic if your own church education is weak and insufficient.*

It's all because I became a "friend raiser" not a fundraiser. It's like that classic scene from *It's A Wonderful Life* when George Bailey realizes true wealth comes in powerful connections and relationships. James stated the reason we don't have is because we don't ask (James 4:2). He's right. But you need to know whom to ask and that's where networking and relationships work. It's not that you build relationships to get money—if you're thinking that, you've missed my point greatly. Rather, you build friendships without strings. You create connections and carve community without conditions. You love on people and you give them your time, talent, and even your treasure sometimes. You can't expect to receive what you won't give.

What you may not realize is your congregation is rich in possibilities and wealthy in opportunities. When God owns the cattle on a thousand hills why are you worried about what's for dinner? Where's the beef? It's what's for supper! This was the faith that drove a widow to give her final cents. Even if no one else notices, God will. And even if no one else cares, God does. And even if we can't buy a loaf of bread, God still provides manna for his kids.

Smaller church youth ministry thrives on faith not finances. You don't need temporal money but eternal motivation. God isn't some magic genie or moneymaker, anyway. Sometimes it's in poverty that we realize our riches. Sometimes it's in our scarcity that we uncover treasures like faith, grace, beauty, simplicity, and sacrifice.

Smaller congregations also have great resources through other churches and denominational systems. There is a beauty in borrowing and humility in seeking help.

Many larger congregations possess vast resources in books, videos, curriculum, programming, and equipment. The key is friendship and relationship. Take youth pastors from larger churches to lunch. Don't even talk about needing stuff from them. Just build a friendship. Seek counsel and advice.

Ask what books they're reading on youth ministry or a hot resource that's really working with teenagers. Visit their youth groups and observe what they do. As you grow in relationships, you'll discover they have the same frustrations you do: volunteers, facilities, parents, students, and yes, even money.

What if every smaller church in America linked itself to a larger congregation, not for resources but relationship? You guessed it. The assets would follow the alliance. There's power in people and purpose in priority. Where our hearts dwell, our treasure is found. Simple networking also provides you with opportunities to grow as a youth worker. You'll discover countless area training events; youth worker fellowships and community resources are available.

Julie is a busy youth worker for her church of 85. She runs a local restaurant and serves in several community leadership roles. She doesn't have much time but still believes in giving back to her church, and the youth ministry was a perfect place. Julie already recognized the value in networking. She joined a Toastmaster Club to improve her speaking and leadership skills. One day, after the club meeting was over, Bob approached her and inquired about her work. After a few minutes she realized he ran a local print shop and did website development on the side (a business venture he was trying to get off the ground).

Julie wanted to develop a website for the youth group but had no time or money for the work.

Bob was equally impressed with Julie's food business and offered her a trade of services. Within a couple months the youth ministry had a vibrant and cool website due to Julie's connection in the community. That's the potency in networking! It reveals that resources are everywhere and relationships are the plug to empower fresh insights and ideas.

The problem for many, if not most, smaller church youth ministries is ecclesiastical myopia (narrow-vision) and ignorance (narrow-mindedness). We choose to cloister and close ourselves off from larger congregations and community connections.

In the 21st century, a flat cyber world creates countless low-cost and no-cost opportunities. In fact, many futurists see a world where "free" is a common marketing tactic. In the future, musicians will record and distribute music complimentary (it's already happening in China) and make their living through concerts and special appearances. Digitization has continually shown itself to lower prices even down to free. Many publishing houses and youth ministry sites already have free downloads. It's possible you're reading this book right now as a digital work—that you got for free.

Smaller churches and their youth ministries will enjoy fresh advantages in such a cyber culture. Resources will be available with a simple mouse click. Access to counsel and consultation is only a website away. It's already happening. Check out the Simply Youth Ministry podcast on iTunes. You'll find for free all sorts of helpful insights and ideas.

Finally, tap into the faith of the widow. With God even the smallest plug nickel has value.

Just like his eye is on the sparrow he won't let your work crash in vain. Your plans may not turn out like you envisioned and you might have to change lanes or crank a U-turn, but that's OK.

Just smile that you're in a beat-up Toyota. Then pop the top down, turn up the radio, and enjoy the ride as you leave all those tractor-trailers in the dust.

Steph's 2-Cents

So let's get down to the core of the biggest problem for a smaller church's youth worker. Find yourself working too many hours on too small a budget with too few resources, too high expectations, and too little compensation? If you find yourself between this particular rock and hard place, here are a few practical ideas to make it all stretch:

"Too Little Money"

Over the years, I've met small church youth directors who were SO excited to find a youth position, they told their churches, "Just pay me what you can." I don't know a single one of them who stayed very long at that church. Do yourself and your church a favor: Know what you're talking about by arming yourself with research on comparable pay/benefits for similar jobs out in the marketplace. Check out salaries and benefits for local schoolteachers. Also be prepared to show your church's hiring committee a set of guidelines for expectations and salary compensation from other churches.

The best tool? Use Group's "Youth Ministry Salary Survey"—it's released every other year—as your weapon of choice for what's happening in youth workers' compensation packages across the country. Read it and KEEP it. You'll need it one day!

I know what you're thinking. "My church just doesn't have the money to pay me more." Or, how about this: "Paid?

What are you talking about? I've been the volunteer youth director for five years!" I get that.

Here are other forms of compensation to supplement your income or at least offset personal expenses:

1. **Free meals:** According to my checkbook, it seems like my church has a dinner every other day. Maybe your church can offer you (and your family?) a "free ticket" to the dinners so you can still be a part of the fellowship without the frequent out-of-pocket expenses.

2. **Gadget budget:** Make sure your church is prepared to reimburse you for all those crazy MUST HAVE props (like smelly-markers, marshmallows, and other items of mayhem) that every youth worker needs to make youth stuff happen.

3. **All expenses paid:** If your church can't pay you the salary you need, make sure they pay you for the cost of all youth events. Whether the funds come from the church budget or a member/benefactor, it will keep you from going broke from all those go-carts rides and movie nights.

4. **Holidays off:** Give you all the national holidays off. A nice little perk churches can give a part-timer. Doesn't really cost your church a thing but sends the message they care.

"Too Few Resources"

Like Rick said, a small church may think it's ready to hire a youth director, figures the salary into the overall church budget, but then doesn't allow anything for a youth budget. It's like getting a new car and then having no money for gas.

If a church is ready to pay someone, then the church MUST be able to front the budget to go along with it. Don't know how to budget?

Here's a tried and true formula that's worked for me:

1. **Summer Trips:** Your budget should cover at least the cost of you and a person of the opposite sex to go on your group's annual summer trip. As the group grows in size, so should the amount of appropriate coverage for adults to attend. Start off with $1,000 for two people.

2. **Fun Events:** Even if your group is small, you have to take yourself and another person everywhere the group goes, so budget for two adults (minimum) to go wherever it is your group goes. To average it all out, how about $10 x two people each month.

3. **Basic Youth Director Needs:** Budget for a year's subscription to Group Magazine, enough money to buy two new written resources a month, a monthly subscription to Napster (and downloads), your cell phone, and gas money. A good computer goes without saying.

4. **Per Youth:** From this point on, the math gets fuzzier but I would say request at least $1,000 per youth currently active in your group. This amount covers all the other stuff involved like supplies, curriculum costs, and so on.

"Ten Ways to S-t-r-e-t-c-h Your Resources"

1. **iTunes vs. new CDs:** I've found my Napster subscription a good investment. It gives me the chance to listen to each track and then pay for only the downloads I want or need.

2. **Supply depot:** Find one central place in your church where everyone in ministry can share supplies. It helps cut down on "double buying" stuff like scissors, balloons, streamers, and other resources.

3. **Area youth library:** Get a youth worker in your area to host a "shared" youth ministry resource library. My shelves are full of studies and books I only needed once. Sharing is good!

4. **Save on gas—van pool:** If you know of other groups going to the same event or location as your group, why not fill up any empty seats by traveling together? It's also fun!

5. **Share your special events:** Share any special speakers, entertainment, or workshops. If you can't host these events together (which is the ultimate way to save) then share on the expenses of bringing someone in—two events for the price of one!

6. **Know your church members:** Save by getting to know your church members' hobbies and careers. Find the "geek squad" member in your church. See who travels a lot and has frequent-flier miles to donate.

7. **Bundle your church's tech needs:** Maybe you're the savviest techno geek on your church staff so help your church save by bundling all your connection needs. The more you help them save, the better the stewardship.

8. **Job share:** If you know of churches near each other that are looking for part-time youth workers, suggest they pool their resources with a job share. They'll get more "more ministry for their money"—you! The payoff for you is increased hours and compensation.

9. **Tax exemption:** Make sure anyone shopping for your ministry's needs is equipped with a copy of your church's tax certificate so money isn't wasted on paying taxes for otherwise tax-free stuff. It adds up!

10. **Free food:** Plan ahead so you can let church members know your group's food needs. There are always people in your church willing to "donate cookies to the cause."

We all have pastimes, interests, and hobbies.

For me, I like to travel and eat. Several years ago I decided my various journeys would include the pursuit of extraordinary, obscure, and "locally famous" eateries. Unlike conventional fast food and dining franchises that dot many American communities, I wanted to find those exceptional one-of-a-kind or uniquely small and specialized places.

That's how I found Lambert's Café, just outside Springfield, Missouri. One of four restaurants nationally, Lambert's is wholly unique, down-home hillbilly cuisine. Your meal comes in a frying pan and you dine off brown paper towels. Servers walk the restaurant aisles offering complimentary side items like fried okra, macaroni, and fried potatoes. But stay alert! Hot rolls also whiz around the room, tossed to expectant diners with uncanny accuracy. Dip your bread in sorghum and order the hen-cut chicken-fried steak for a dining experience you won't soon forget.

Every time I travel to California my first stop is In-N-Out Burger. This "fast food" joint betrays that moniker given to today's processed, frozen, freeze-dried, and "heat lamp" strategies used by most franchises. In-N-Out is the quintessential California burger, fries, and shake combo, completely made to order using only fresh 100 percent beef, peeled potatoes, and ice cream. If you're a fan, you even know the "secret menu" for burger orders like "Animal Style" or "Flying Dutchman." Unlike other chains that exploded nationally and now globally, In-N-Out has remained faithful to original core values and careful, even overly cautious, expansion. For years Southern California was the only place you could find In-N-Out, but recently it has grown into Las Vegas, Arizona, Utah, and other parts of California—much to the delight of In-N-Out fans.

For pizza fanatics check out Little Big Man's in Montana or Valentino's in Nebraska. For ice cream you can't go wrong with chocolate chip mint at Graeter's in Cincinnati or a Ted Drewes "concrete" in St. Louis. For barbeque it's Jack Stack's in Kansas City. I've also dined at countless places

I no longer recall, though the experience remains, including a downtown country western pub in Nashville, Tennessee; a fish and chips joint in Seaside, Oregon; and a cook-your-own-steak house in Norfolk, Virginia. In Eagle, Idaho, you'll find a converted church coffee shop known as Rembrandts that hands down is the place to drink Joe in the Treasure Valley.

If I've learned anything from these dining experiences it's the emotional connection that emerges. I remember the food was great, but what I truly retain is the feeling. I enjoyed the moment. I felt something that I can't shake. Maybe it's sipping sweet tea in the Deep South on a sweltering summer day or a "milky way mocha" in the Great Northwest during the dead of winter. Maybe it's the pumpkin shake that's locally produced and sold through Burgervilles only found in western Oregon or 25-cent cones at Little America in Wyoming. And if you haven't been to Casa Bonita in Denver you're missing out. It's not the greatest food, but few restaurants can transport you into a south-of-the-border villa with a pool and waterfall, mariachi bands, cliff divers, caves to explore, and countless other forms of fun.

What's my point?

Smaller church youth ministries grow around personal and powerful experiences. You don't need to adopt big franchise chain strategies to succeed. Sometimes, like In-N-Out you simply need to hold true to values that make you unique, fresh, and 100 percent true. Maybe you simply need to create a fun place to experience God, like Lambert's. Take your Bible studies to a different level. Focus on a few side helpings and keep tossing surprises that make the kids hunger for more. Maybe you'll be one-of-a-kind like Casa Bonita or Rembrandts. You might not make much noise by the world's standards, but kids who graduate will spread the word that you made an eternal difference.

As with most things I write, I never know how to finish. If you've journeyed with Stephanie and me this far, I pray that you've been encouraged, inspired, and motivated to think differently. Smaller is taller. It's advantageous to drive a Toyota not a tractor-trailer in heavy traffic. Don't count the kids; make the kids count.

All of these messages will hopefully continue to ring throughout your work with teenagers in your smaller church.

I also hope you'll continue this conversation online. Feel free to write Stephanie or me with your questions, comments, or concerns. We both care deeply for you and your congregation.

Let me simply leave you with this final thought. Too many times we misunderstand "success" in life and ministry. Too often we focus on the splash (size, noise, immediate impact) that we make when in reality we should reflect on the reach of the ripples.

You may only touch one kid in your ministry, but that one teenager may one day become an influential leader, communicator, media personality, or celebrity. If God wills and blesses, you will undoubtedly impact far more than one. Your splash can ripple for eternity. And don't forget that you can't skip stones with boulders. Small still is tall!

You'll never know the reach of your work in this life, but eventually you'll witness the ripples. You'll hear the words of a grateful God saying "well done." You'll enjoy testimonies of students, parents, church leaders, and neighbors who extol your faithfulness. You'll one day experience the difference you made.

So make a splash. It doesn't matter how big.

Then watch God ripple!

Dr. Rick Chromey: rickchromey@gmail.com
Stephanie Caro: THEEMQUEEN@aol.com

NOTES